Greenhill Books

MEMOIRS OF NAPOLEON'S EGYPTIAN EXPEDITION, 1798–1801

MEMOIRS OF NAPOLEON'S EGYPTIAN EXPEDITION 1798–1801

by Captain Joseph-Marie Moiret
of the 75^e Demi-Brigade

Translated and Edited by Rosemary Brindle

Greenhill Books, London
Stackpole Books, Pennsylvania

Memoirs of Napoleon's Egyptian Expedition, 1798–1801
first published 2001 by Greenhill Books, Lionel Leventhal Limited, Park House,
1 Russell Gardens, London NW11 9NN
www.greenhillbooks.com
and
Stackpole Books, 5067 Ritter Road, Mechanicsburg, PA 17055, USA

British Library Cataloguing in Publication Data available

ISBN 1-85367-449-4

Library of Congress Cataloging-in-Publication Data available

Publishing History
Captain Joseph-Marie Moiret's memoirs were first published as *Mémoires sur l'Expédition
d'Egypte* (Paris, 1984). *Memoirs of Napoleon's Egyptian Expedition, 1798–1801* is a translation
of the French edition, with the addition of new material compiled by the translator,
including an introduction, maps, short biographies, and a sixteen-page plate section.

Typeset by DP Photosetting
Printed and bound in Great Britain by CPD (Wales), Ebbw Vale

CONTENTS

CONTENTS

CHAPTER XI

SHORT BIOGRAPHIES

LIST OF ILLUSTRATIONS

9

INTRODUCTION

The French Campaign in Egypt
by Rosemary Brindle, translator and editor

In 1818, a well-known publisher of the period, a Monsieur Moriceau, prepared the memoirs of Captain Moiret for publication. They were not published at that time, however; the reason for this is not known, but they might well have been considered politically sensitive, as it was not until that year that allied troops were finally withdrawn from French soil, and the French people were still exhausted by the turmoil and bloodshed of the past decades. Publication earlier would have risked the anger of Imperial censors, giving as it does too frank and truthful a picture of the Emperor.

Descendants of Captain Moiret emigrated to Argentina, and it was to be more than a hundred years before these recollections of the young captain were to be published in France, following the purchase of the manuscript at a sale of his family archives in Buenos Aires.

Few facts are known about Joseph-Marie Moiret himself. He was born of a good family with connections to the aristocracy, at Courtenay in Dauphiné, and studied classics with the scholarly curé of a nearby village with a view to becoming a priest. He entered the college of the Dominican Fathers at Lyon as a student of philosophy but did not complete his studies.

He seems to have suffered the early loss of his mother, like so many others of that period when death in child-birth was common, and he longed to leave his father's house, where his step-mother made him feel unwelcome. One day a recruiting sergeant for the Aquitaine Regiment met the young man in Lyon, overcame any objections he might have had, and enrolled him in the corps.

Moiret was to remain faithful to the corps and to the friends he made in it until the end of his military career. He and his comrades regarded it as a point of honour to serve together under the same flag, and pledged themselves never to separate even at the cost of the promotion which transfer to a larger formation might have offered.

Following his recruitment, Moiret progressed quickly through the ranks until, at the outbreak of war in Savoy, at the start of the Revolution, he was a non-commissioned officer of the regiment under the command of General

Montesquiou. The rapid expansion of the Revolutionary Army produced further promotion and at the time of the Egyptian expedition he was a supply officer with the rank of captain. We do not know where this promotion was won, but his regiment, the 75th Demi-Brigade, certainly distinguished itself in the Italian campaign, where it earned the title 'The Invincible'.

The Memoirs briefly shine a vivid light on the Captain and on an extraordinary episode in French history; an episode which has come to be seen as a side-show of the Napoleonic wars, but which had far-reaching cultural and political repercussions. From the beginning, aboard a troop-ship in Toulon Harbour in May 1798, until his return home to quarantine at Marseilles in November 1801 the captain watches and notes. He records his experiences using any writing materials which come to hand under active service conditions; he sometimes finds it necessary to use home-made ink with a reed for a pen. He reports the oratorical words of the Commander-in-Chief in full, but his own style is always simple and direct. He is senior enough and experienced enough to appreciate the plans of the Staff, but near enough to the troops to hear their grumbles and understand their sufferings, which he shares. Only very occasionally does his own anger and bewilderment find a voice. He seems to have been very much a man of his period, intelligent and enquiring, an interesting product of a pre-Revolutionary upbringing modified by the Republican ideas of the 'Enlightenment'. He was, above all, a French patriot.

The Egyptian expedition of which Joseph–Marie Moiret found himself a part was, perhaps, the coincidence of Napoleon's two interests – war and science – the realisation of an ambition to demonstrate in one brilliant stroke his mastery of both, and to emulate his heroes Alexander and Newton. He was quoted later by the poet Népomucène Lemercier as saying:

> Had I not become a Commanding General I should have embraced the study of science. My path would have been that of Galileo and Newton. And, as I have always succeeded in my undertakings, so then I should have become very distinguished in the world of science. I should have left behind the legacy of great discoveries. No other glory could have tempted my ambition.

This typically bombastic remark was hardly supported by Bonaparte's actual knowledge of matters scientific at any time, but indicates his conviction of his ability. There can be no doubt that, among the honours heaped upon him as a successful general, none was more valued by Napoleon than the friendship and respect of men of science. He came to believe that Egypt would be the stage on which his ambition could be realised.

His proposal was to force his way into Egypt, using a combination of military might and propaganda, conquer the country for France and at the same time, by means of the Scientific Commission he would take with him, recreate in the manner of the Enlightenment the ancient civilisation, so long crushed under Turkish rule.

Such a venture would be timely. Appointed as Commander-in-Chief of the Army of England on his return from Italy in December 1797, Bonaparte was quickly convinced that disaster would result from an invasion attempt while the Royal Navy controlled the Channel. He well knew that reputations under the Republic were as easily lost as won and that his aura of invincibility must not be put at risk. His ambition needed the fuel of more military success to maintain the momentum of his career: victory in Egypt seemed to risk little and to promise much. The conqueror and civiliser of a new province for France would be assured of the glory for which Napoleon felt himself to be destined.

The idea of an invasion of Egypt was not new. The Duc de Choiseul in the time of Louis XV had suggested that Egypt could become a colony to compensate France for her losses in North America, but in the next reign the Comte de Vergennes, then ambassador of France in Constantinople, had answered a complaint from the French Vice-Consul in Alexandria about an Egyptian official by writing, 'We have more valuable interests to guard in Turkey than to risk burying an army in the sands of Egypt.' [Amis de Malmaison] In 1798, however, other considerations unfortunately prevailed and the traditional alliance between France and Turkey fell victim to expedience.

Napoleon had a powerful advocate in his effort to convince the French Government of the value of his Egyptian scheme. Talleyrand, then Minister for Foreign Affairs, supported the idea. The Ottoman Empire gave every sign of breaking up, and its hold on Egypt was weak. The moment appeared to have come when France might move to take advantage of its old ally's weakness and seize control of a desirable colony. It was understood that Talleyrand was to go as Ambassador to Constantinople where he would persuade the Sultan to accept the French invasion of Egypt as a friendly act, which would rid the country of the Mameluks, who effectively ruled and who paid only a minimal homage to the Sultan who was the titular ruler. In the event, Talleyrand made no such journey to Constantinople, and the Sublime Porte was to resent forcefully the French invasion of his province. Napoleon, many years later and perhaps with this in mind, referred to Talleyrand as 'merde dans un bas de soie'. [Cooper]

The five Directors forming the government of the time were also aware that their precarious position would be less threatened at home if this dangerously popular, victorious general were removed from the admiring Parisian mob, and despatched to a land from which he might never return, or at least return with damaged reputation. Perhaps the most important factor in reaching the final decision was that Napoleon himself had determined upon the expedition to Egypt, and could not be denied. Bourrienne[1] later wrote that 'The Directory was as uninvolved, as regards its personal inclination, in the departure of Bonaparte [for Egypt] as in his return. It was only the passive agent of Bonaparte's wishes'.

The fact that the army so recently victorious in Italy was now available for the Egyptian venture also appealed to the increasingly unpopular Directors. It was an army devoted to Napoleon, one which had set out for Italy ragged and unpaid and had returned with millions of francs in gold and even more in treasure. It might even, given the turbulence of the times, be used to threaten the weak and divided government. There were other considerations too. Conquered, Egypt could prove a stepping-stone to triumph in the Far East and the appropriation of the lucrative trade hitherto enjoyed by the British. In furtherance of this aim a letter was sent by Bonaparte to Tippoo Sahib, the Sultan of Mysore and the inveterate enemy of the British in India, proposing, on the principal of 'my enemy's enemy is my friend', a joint effort by Indian and French armies with the aim of throwing the British out of the sub-continent.

The collection of the artists and scientists to form the Commission which was to measure, catalogue, describe and explore the whole of Egypt was largely the work of two eminent men who had sponsored Napoleon's election to the French National Institute in December 1797. They were the mathematician Gaspard Monge and the chemist Claude Berthollet. They took less than two months to persuade, convince and enrol one-hundred and sixty-seven members of the scientific community to embark on this expedition into the unknown. There were chemists, mathematicians, astronomers, engineers, naturalists, mining engineers, architects, artists, writers and printers. Every field of enquiry was covered: boat-builders were included, as were builders of roads and bridges, zoologists as well as economists, cartographers and geologists. It is a source of wonder that so many of the intellectual elite were found who were prepared to risk everything on what must, at best, have seemed to be a gamble. Monge himself, who was fifty-one and twice the average age of those on the Commission, certainly hesitated about going, but his friendship for Napoleon and the persuasion of Berthollet, only two years his junior, were powerful factors in

---

[1] Louis Antoine Fauvelet de Bourrienne (1769–1834), Napoleon's school fellow and, subsequently, his Secretary from 1797 to 1804.

his decision. The glamour and apparent invincibility of the Command-ing General must have worked its magic on the others too.

Dominique Vivant Denon, whose engravings were later published in the 'Description of Egypt', which was to provide a lasting justification for the expedition, said 'One word from the hero who commanded the Expedition determined my departure; he promised to take me with him and I had no doubt of my safe return.' [Dhombres]

Such unquestioning faith in Napoleon was, however, not sufficient for some of the younger members, amongst whom a variety of motives played their part. Jean Baptiste Prosper Jollois was only twenty-two – the average age of the Commission was twenty-five – and he was frank about his rea-sons for the journey. 'First, the wish to travel, then the burning desire to learn, to experience; finally the deep conviction that the journey would be of use to me.' [Dhombres] Added inducements were material: his salary would be paid by the Ecole Polytechnique, from which he had recently graduated, as well as his expenses. His grade as engineer would be granted when the expedition set out and he would be assured of a civil service position on his return. It would be wrong, however, to discount idealism as a motive impelling at least some of this gathering of young men. Repub-licanism and the ideas of the Enlightenment were still powerful forces in 1798. Many of these young men, even with no idea of their destination, must have placed their trust in the patriotism of their leaders to make the glory of France their goal.

Indeed the ostensible object of the expedition was to free the land of Egypt from oppressive Ottoman rule. This was to be achieved at no expense to France; the funds to cover the cost of the first few months had been confiscated from the treasury of Berne when the Republican armies overran the Swiss Federation, and thereafter the 'liberated' Egyptians were destined to pay for their own liberation by means of taxes collected by the French Army, which they would also supply with food. Napoleon's tactics, the rapidity of manoeuvre that had been so successful in the past, had largely depended upon the army's ability to 'live off the land'. Once more it was intended that the invaded would pay for their invasion.

This concept, which had worked so well in relatively rich Europe, contained the seeds of disaster in poverty-stricken Egypt as it was later to do in Russia. Shoddy logistics and undefended lines of communication were to load the dice too heavily against a Commander-in-Chief so dependent upon luck.

Once the huge fleet of battleships and transports in the ports of Toulon and Civita Veccia began to gather, speed of action was essential. It was impossible to disguise from the British that something of great importance was in hand, but the destination of the armada was a closely guarded secret.

15

The Memoirs give an amusing impression of the bewilderment of the troops crammed in the overcrowded transports, but Moiret hardly mentions the storm which blew the watchful British squadron out to sea and thus permitted the French ships to set off unobserved. It had taken only two months to collect the ships (there were four hundred of them, including thirteen ships of the line), to enrol the members of the Commission and embark the thirty-four thousand land troops as well as about sixteen thousand sailors. It was an almost incredible feat of organisation, but inevitably there were consequences which were to become very apparent as the months passed. Strangely, little consideration seems to have been given to the conditions under which the army would have to operate. The food and water in the transports that carried them across the Mediterranean were inadequate and rotten, and other shortcomings were to become fatally apparent under battle conditions. Landing tactics had not been practised and the exhausted troops, when they at last arrived off Alexandria, were to struggle through the surf in the teeth of a stiff gale. Moiret says nothing of this, but another soldier of higher rank reports 'the sea was very rough, we were covered with spray and most of the troops were very sea-sick ... and in danger from half-submerged rocks on the imperfectly charted coast.' [Doguereau] The problem of getting the cavalry horses ashore had also to be solved on the spot.

The swift capture of Malta and about six million francs' worth of treasure gave the expedition a welcome reward for the weeks of anxiety and discomfort. His delight and surprise at the rapidity of the French victory seems to show that Captain Moiret had no knowledge of the preliminary diplomacy which had ensured the triumph. The Knights of St John of Jerusalem, who were nearly all French, had agreed to accept the lifetime pensions which were offered to them in return for their surrender after only token resistance. The island treasury was stripped and the finest valuables despatched to France aboard the frigate *Sensible* together with important despatches from Napoleon. (Unfortunately, the ship was captured by the British frigate *Sea Horse*.) A small garrison was left to enjoy the charms of the population so vividly described in the Memoirs, and the main body of the expedition sailed away to Egypt.

His legendary good luck gave Napoleon the days he needed to disembark his army and take Alexandria, before the British naval squadron returned there to realise that their slow quarry had been behind them rather than ahead. However, there was very little luck for the Army of Egypt thereafter.

Deficiencies resulting from hasty planning and preparation made themselves apparent as the army struggled from the coast to Cairo. No water containers had been provided, food had to be obtained from the countryside – no easy matter in desert conditions – and the burning sun beat pitilessly upon the hot uniforms of the men carrying heavy equipment. Yet discipline was largely maintained, and there was no lessening of courage in battle, as the Memoirs make clear in the accounts of the battles of Chebreiss and the Pyramids. It was before the latter encounter that Napoleon afterwards claimed to have addressed his troops with the words 'Soldiers, from the height of these pyramids forty centuries look down on you'. Unusually, Moiret does not mention this speech. The battle was a triumph for the disciplined if exhausted French troops but not, perhaps, the decisive victory that Napoleon reported in his despatches to the Directory, for large numbers of the Mameluks escaped. Their leaders fled; Ibrahim Bey fled towards Syria while Murad Bey vanished south into the desert, pursued by General Desaix. Ibrahim had been joint ruler of Egypt with Murad Bey until the incursion of the French, and was again to fight against the invaders at Heliopolis. Murad, another leader of the Mameluk warrior caste, succeeded in evading the pursuing General Desaix with about five thousand mounted soldiers. His loyalties were doubtful – he quarrelled with his Ottoman superiors and when he died of plague in 1801 it was not clear whether he was leading his men to join the French or the British Army.

The French Army was cheered by the victory of the Pyramids, but had little other comfort. They had been promised the conquest of a rich and fertile land and the gratitude of a welcoming population. What they had found was desert, hunger and thirst, stinking villages with impoverished and hostile inhabitants and decayed towns such as Alexandria and Cairo, in which little remained except the ruins of former glory. Even the wells had been poisoned or filled up with sand. Bourrienne reports that 'as soon as the French troops set foot in Egypt they were filled with dissatisfaction and ardently longed to return home. The illusion of the expedition had disappeared and only its reality remained'. He goes on to say that the complaints, even of senior officers were 'often so unmeasured as to amount to sedition'. Disillusioned in the midst of savagery and poverty, the troops wondered if they would survive to enjoy the six acres promised to them by Napoleon on their return to France.

Napoleon entered Cairo on 24th July 1798. On 1st August Admiral Nelson entirely destroyed the French battle fleet off Aboukir Bay. The French were effectively stranded in Egypt, lacking the possibility of reinforcement or retreat.

In August 1798, General Desaix left with about four thousand men in pursuit of Murad Bey. His campaign, which lasted for nearly two years, constituted what might be called a separate war, in which he inflicted heavy casualties on the enemy while sustaining relatively few himself. His military brilliance was firmly established as he contrived with his small army to contain Murad and force his retreat deep into the Sudan. Desaix's men were plagued with illness – notably ophthalmia – as well as shortages of practically everything, which made it impossible to follow up their magnificent victories as they should have done. Lack of ammunition robbed Desaix of complete success. His opinion of Napoleon, poor even in the early days of the Italian campaign ('he is very rich, as well he might be, since he draws on a whole country's revenues ... he believes neither in probity nor decency. He says all this is foolishness'), had not been improved by the failure of the Commander-in-Chief to respond to his demands for rations, medicines and mules during the advance on Cairo with anything more substantial than copies of his proclamation to the Egyptians. [Herald] But nevertheless Desaix and his men fought valiantly for France in Upper Egypt with only the excitement of their amazing archaeological discoveries to cheer them.

Captain Moiret, who remained with General Kléber's division, had no first-hand knowledge of the part of the campaign that took place in Upper Egypt, but he quotes Napoleon's report to the Directory of 19th June 1799, which fills the gap in his own narrative. That report contains an interesting hint of the political agents carried at that time on French ships, presumably to enforce the political correctness of the day. Napoleon's impatience with such gentry is clear!

From the first, by means of his proclamations, Napoleon had claimed that he was the liberator of the Egyptian people from their oppressors, the Mameluks. He declared that the coming of the French was the will of Allah, that a new era of prosperity and justice was about to dawn, when local religions and customs would be respected and government would again be in the hands of the Egyptians themselves.

There was, of course, an obvious contradiction between the actual colonising goal of the conquest of Egypt and the altruistic claims made by Napoleon. Some Egyptians were at first seduced by the prospect of liberation from the tyranny of the Turks, but the reality of the war soon became only too apparent to them. Military imperatives overrode philosophical idealism, for there was at all times an irreconcilable divergence between the aims of the Army and those of the Institute. The almost unbelievable energy displayed by Napoleon in his efforts to set up his own administration following the news of the catastrophe at Aboukir Bay is one of the most remarkable features of the entire campaign. His determination inspired his disillusioned officers and men, and contrived for a while to carry forward the two original aims of the expedition: conquest and scientific discovery.

Although his despatches to the French Government implied otherwise, Napoleon's hold on Egypt was always tenuous; he ruled only where force could be applied, in Cairo and a few other centres. Military rule was imposed on the native population and, when resisted, maintained with a brutality which recalled the revolutionary days of the Terror. At the same time the members of the Commission founded the Egyptian Institute, modelled on the National Institute of France, and began their work. Their aspirations were of the highest kind, and a single-minded pursuit of knowledge marked their endeavours.

Jean-Lambert Tallien, who in France had been a member of the Committee of Public Safety, now became editor of the *Egyptian Decade*, the journal of the new Institute. Probably expressing the genuine hopes of the members of the Commission, Tallien wrote in the first number of the four-page paper:

> This conquest must not be of use politically and commercially to France alone. Science and the Arts must gain from it. We no longer live in times when victors spread only destruction wherever they go, greed for gold determines their actions and devastation, persecution and intolerance are their companions. Today, by contrast, the French respect not only the laws, customs and conventions, but even the prejudices of those whose countries they occupy. It is left to time, reason and education to bring about those changes for which philosophy and the enlightenment of the century have prepared the way, and which every day come nearer.

Scientists, artists and technologists studied every aspect of the country. Its natural history, geology and archaeology were examined, catalogued and where appropriate sketched and measured. However, the stranded army also had need of their help. Committees of scientists and technicians were formed to study ways of supplying deficiencies in food and material resulting from the British blockade which denied supply ships access to Egyptian ports. Napoleon instructed the Commission to discover ways of baking sufficient bread for the army and to determine urgently a method of manufacturing gunpowder from local resources.

Everything was achieved against a background of continual danger, disease and difficulty. As early as 13th August 1798 the first casualties had occurred among the Commission members: one of the artists, Joly, while accompanying a reconnaissance under General Menou, was killed at the village of Cafr'Schabbas Ammer, and the orientalist Panhusen, acting as General Kléber's interpreter, vanished in Alexandria, presumably killed by Arabs. Perhaps the most serious loss of all was that of Simon Antoine Sucy, head of the Army's administration, who had been severely wounded at the Battle of the Pyramids. Wishing to return to France, he embarked at Alexandria together with two hundred wounded soldiers. When their ship put in to Sicily to take on fresh water they were attacked by the inhabitants and murdered. Another member of the Commission, a doctor, Daburon, is also recorded as having died in Sicily at the same time. It seems likely that he had been sent on the same ship to care for the wounded during the voyage, and had suffered the same fate as Sucy. Sucy's place in the political economy section of the Egyptian Institute was filled by Bourrienne.

In pursuit of his aim of appearing to allow the Egyptians to govern their own country, Napoleon instituted Divans, Councils composed of local sheikhs. These were of course his own appointees, dependant on his goodwill and recipients of lavish gifts. ('We must give these people leaders, or they will choose their own,' he wrote. [Amis de Malmaison]) To further conciliate them Napoleon began to profess his esteem for Islam. He implied that he was on the point of conversion to that faith and that he would bring the whole French Army with him. (Bourrienne denies that the General ever learned or repeated any Koranic verses, but also adds 'I will not go so far as to say that he would not have changed his religion had the conquest of the East been the price of that change.') Yet, after the first revolt in Cairo, Napoleon was to write to one of his generals 'Every night we have about thirty heads chopped off, many of them belonging to the ringleaders. This I believe will serve them as a good lesson'. [Herald] In addition, incensed by the incidence of venereal disease among the soldiers, he caused hundreds of prostitutes to be rounded up and decapitated. Following the Cairo uprising, the situation of the French looked disastrous. Disease and unrest were rife in the ranks of the Army, and the population remained hostile so that individuals and small groups dared not move freely even in the towns. Boredom was becoming the enemy of discipline, and many officers sought to return to France. It also became clear that the Turkish Sultan was on the point of invading Egypt through Syria. Napoleon, while maintaining to the Directory that all was well ('we lack nothing here. We are full of strength, good health and high spirits', he wrote [Herald]), determined to strike first and conquer Syria to pre-empt the Turkish invasion. A realistic appraisal of his position, cut off as he was from supplies and reinforcements, makes it hard to believe that the Commander-in-Chief still dreamed of a triumphant advance on Constantinople and a further march to India. He may have hoped that success would enable him to recruit an army from amongst the Christian Arabs. At about the time that the expedition to Syria was being prepared,

An Indian arrived at Suez, declaring himself to be an envoy from Tippoo Sahib. He came to Cairo to see Bonaparte. He no longer carried any despatches; he said that those given to him by the prince to hand to Bonaparte had been stolen by the Arabs into whose hands he had fallen near Djeddah. He affirmed that Tippoo Sahib was making great preparations and counted on the arrival of the French, looking forward to alliance with Bonaparte. [Doguereau]

In his memoirs, Napoleon later suggested that he might have continued to India and founded an Asiatic empire, but his decision to take an army into Syria to overcome the Turkish threat must primarily have resulted from a concern to seize the initiative and obtain the benefit of surprise. Nevertheless he wrote again to Tippoo Sahib:

> You are of course already informed of my arrival on the banks of the Red Sea with a numerous and invincible army. Eager to deliver you from the iron yoke of England, I hasten to request that you will send me, by way of Mascate or Mocha, an account of the political situation in which you are. [Bourrienne]

The Syrian expedition was a disastrous waste of courage and good troops. Captain Moiret gives a vivid account of the torments of thirst and hunger experienced by the Army on its way to El Arich, where he was wounded and forced to remain while his division continued under General Kléber to Gaza, Jaffa and finally to St Jean-d'Acre.

In spite of his wound and his subsequent illness, some would count Captain Moiret fortunate, for he was one of very few to recover from the plague as well as being spared some of the horrors which accompanied the rest of the Syrian campaign.

Napoleon seized Gaza, and took possession of vast stores of gunpowder and other munitions as well as supplies of food, thus helping to counteract the fact that his army had been hastily prepared for the expedition and was ill-supplied. It must have seemed at this point that Bonaparte's legendary luck was still with him. A staff officer wrote,

> One has to admire Bonaparte's good fortune. Without pre-prepared stores, he crosses an enormous desert and takes El-Arich at the moment his troops run out of provisions. Biscuit found at El-Arich takes us to Gaza where the enemy had stock-piled warehouses and had the stupidity to abandon them to us without either defending or destroying them. Arriving at Ramleh and Lydda with these supplies we find yet more storehouses. Finally Jaffa gives us enough provisions of all sorts to take us on to Acre. (Unpublished journal held by *Archives Historiques de la Guerre*.)

Jaffa put up a sturdier opposition than El Arich, but a brief siege ended in the massacre of the Turkish garrison, followed by rape and murder as troops ran wild in the streets and sacked the town.

> For twenty-four hours the town was given over to the horrors of war. It is impossible to describe a more horrible scene; the roads were heaped with corpses; children were to be seen, murdered in their mothers' arms, and everywhere the shrieks of women whose husbands had been slain. [Doguereau]

In the houses and cellars and towers were found four thousand of Djezzar's troops. These were taken as prisoners of war and guarded for twenty-four hours, then, in one of the most disgraceful episodes of the campaign, they were conducted to the seashore and shot. The reason for this appalling action by Napoleon was alleged to be that the army was short of food and had no other course of action, but ample stores had been found in Jaffa itself, and there were several small ships in the port which could have been utilised to convey the prisoners to Damiette. This was a particularly horrible affair because Bonaparte's aides-de-camp, Eugène de Beauharnais and Croisier, had been active in persuading the defenders of Jaffa to surrender in return for their safety.

As if in retribution plague now struck the French Army with redoubled force. Those members of the Commission who had attached themselves to the Army of Syria suffered along with the troops. The unfortunate Saint-Simon, until recently a Knight of the Order of Saint John, died of plague at Jaffa, as did the engineer Louis Bodard and a lieutenant of engineers, Jean-Balthazar Bringuier, who was also a member of the Commission in the geographical section.

Some effort had been made to conceal from the troops the nature of the disease afflicting them; Napoleon thought that fear itself caused the disease to spread more rapidly; he even spent an hour and a half at the plague hospital in an attempt to improve the morale of his troops. When the army finally marched away from Jaffa, a small garrison was left behind with *Adjudant-Général* Grézieu[2] in command and three hundred plague victims remaining in the hospital. Within three days Grézieu was dead of the illness and a member of the Commission, Etienne-Louis Malus, took charge of the plague hospital. Malus, a mathematician of note, wrote:

> For ten days I went there assiduously and spent every morning in the loathsome stench of that cloaca every corner of which was crowded with patients. It was only on the eleventh day that I noticed the symptoms of the plague. This was about the time when *Adjudant-Général* Grézieu died. Half the garrison already had been stricken by then. About thirty men died every day ... about one man among twelve stricken survived ... The plague was in every house in town ... The monks of the Capuchin monastery quarantined themselves to avoid contagion. Almost all of them died.

Malus himself became infected but was among the minority who recovered from the disease. There was a mortality rate of about ninety percent of plague victims during the Syrian campaign. The work of one of the members of the Commission was especially remarkable at this time. The

---

[2] Pierre Joseph Bérardier, known as Grézieu (1755–1799). *Adjudant-Général* was a rank on the general staff equating to Brigade Commander.

Chief Medical Officer, Desgenettes,[3] whose study of the work of Sir John Pringle, 'Observations on the Diseases of the Army' (published in 1752), had prepared him for the tasks which were to face him throughout the Syrian campaign, became celebrated for his struggles against the plague and the dysentery afflicting the troops. It is of interest that, at a meeting of the Egyptian Institute following his return from Syria, Napoleon crossed swords verbally with Desgenettes. A committee had been appointed to conduct a study of the plague and Desgenettes was on this committee; Napoleon made clear his wish that, in its report, the committee would find that the plague had been responsible for the failure of the Syrian expedition. Desgenettes refused to agree to any such finding and gave his reasons. An acrimonious argument took place to the embarrassment of the assembly, at the end of which Desgenettes said, with some courage,

> I know, citizen ... I know, General, ... since you wish to be something other than a member of the Institute now, I know that I have been forced to say, with some heat, things which will have repercussions far from here; but I will not retract a single word. [Dhombres]

It is to Bonaparte's credit that there is no evidence to indicate that he bore any grudge against Desgenettes for this forthright speech.

To the fear of this horrible illness was added the torture of thirst, ophthalmia, wounds and the ever present terror of the plundering bands of hostile Arabs, as the main body of the army marched on towards Acre, leaving the rotting corpses of the slaughtered Turks on the seashore. The capture of Acre was vital to the French, as it was the only fortified city on the route to Constantinople where the Royal Navy would be able to supply the defenders.

Although the ancient fortifications of the city were dilapidated, the Turkish forces under the Pasha, Djezzar – also known as 'The Butcher' – had certain advantages. Most importantly, the siege guns arriving from Cairo by sea for the French Army had been captured by British ships under Captain Sir Sidney Smith. Smith, with enormous energy, proceeded to direct the rebuilding of the fortifications and the defences of Acre with the expert assistance of Colonel Louis Phélippeaux,[4] a French Royalist officer and one-time classmate of Napoleon at Brienne. The Turks were rallied and supported by a British landing party whose gun-crews were deployed around the walls; guns of the British ships off-shore were brought to bear

---

[3] Nicolas René Dufriche Desgenettes (1762–1837), Physician-in-Chief to the Egyptian Expedition (see also Appendix 2).
[4] Louis Edmond Le Picard de Phélippeaux (1768–1799); slightly different spellings of his surname may be encountered (see Short Biographies).

on the attackers and on their reinforcements arriving along the shore. The French mounted attack after attack at terrible loss to themselves; the siege lasted ten weeks and in that time four generals of the besieging army were killed, including Napoleon's friend, the engineer, Caffarelli.[5] Twelve hundred French soldiers died in the fighting while another thousand were victims of the plague; twice as many were sick or wounded.

The stubborn resistance of the Turks, aware of the dreadful fate of their compatriots at Jaffa and encouraged by the energy and discipline of the British sailors, prevailed and Acre did not fall. At last, and in spite of his victory over a Turkish army at Mount Tabor, Napoleon lifted the siege of Acre and the long weary retreat to Cairo began on 11th May 1799. The horror of this retreat, the disillusionment of the troops and the suffering of the sick and wounded abandoned to die on the way are made clear in Moiret's memoirs. The Captain accepts the burning of crops and villages as a necessity of war. His justified pride in his brigade remains, but there is a change of tone. His attitude is no longer that of unquestioning admiration for his Commander-in-Chief; he writes of the 'unbelievable credulity' of the Egyptians in accepting Napoleon's version of events in Syria.

A 'triumphal' entry into Cairo was made on 14th June. The army had some difficulty in making itself presentable for this ceremony.

> Although we wore our best, we had a miserable air; we lacked everything . . . most of us had neither hats nor boots, or at least what we had was in the worst possible state. [Doguereau]

The Turkish Army which Napoleon had claimed he had destroyed in Syria now landed at Aboukir but was immediately attacked and routed by the French. Following this encounter, copies of British newspapers, kindly provided by Sir Sidney Smith, informed Napoleon of the military reverses which had struck France. Austrian armies under the Archduke Charles were sweeping the French back through Germany even as the Russians succeeded in driving them from Italy. France was in crisis and Napoleon knew that his opportunity to seize power had come. Without even informing the unfortunate General Kléber, his designated successor, of his intentions, he embarked with a chosen few of his generals and his friends, Monge and Berthollet, and left for France on 23rd August 1799, never to return to Egypt.

The army inherited by Kléber was not only diminished by battle casualties and disease but demoralised, surrounded by a hostile population and threatened by Turkish and British forces. It was also unpaid. In a bitter

---

[5] Louis Marie Joseph Maximilien Caffarelli du Falga (1756–1799) (see also Appendix 2).

despatch to the government in Paris, Kléber complained of Napoleon's desertion, but by the time the despatch reached France, the Directory had been overthrown, Bonaparte had installed himself as First Consul, and Kléber was dead.

Pragmatically, in his impossible situation, the gallant Kléber did what he could to alleviate the sufferings of the army. He negotiated what he conceived to be an honourable agreement with Sir Sidney Smith and the Grand Vizier whereby the French Army would be returned to France with its weapons in Turkish transports, but the Convention of El Arich was not ratified in London. Thereafter, with his abandoned army decimated by disease and death, Kléber again led his desperate troops against the Turks, winning a significant victory at Heliopolis. The death, at the hand of a fanatical assassin, of this remarkable general was a final blow to the morale of the army. General Menou, who succeeded to the command by seniority, did not enjoy the respect accorded his predecessor and certainly had none of the almost mystic appeal of Napoleon. He had shown himself to be an irresolute soldier when on 4th October 1795, at the head of a column entrusted with the task of disarming an insurrection, he had simply withdrawn when the rebels refused to disperse. Menou alone among senior officers had actually embraced Islam and married an Egyptian woman, causing the army to suspect that his zeal to return to France might be limited. Although Captain Moiret finds good things to say about him as an administrator, his actions as an army commander were disastrous and bitterly resented by officers under his command. As Moiret recounts, two experienced generals, Reynier and Damas,[6] were returned to France following Menou's attempt to blame them for the defeat by the British near Alexandria on 30th March. At this battle the British commander General Abercromby[7] was killed, as were the French generals Lanusse[8] and Baudot,[9] while General Roize[10] died later of his wounds. Two-thirds of the French force involved were destroyed.

Menou capitulated on 30th August 1801 to a British expeditionary force under General Hutchinson[11] who had succeeded Abercromby to the command, following a series of engagements during which the French forces had become fatally divided both physically and morally.

---

[6] Jean Louis Ebenezer Reynier (1771–1814) (see Short Biographies); François Etienne Damas (1764–1828).

[7] General Sir Ralph Abercromby (1734–1801), mortally wounded at Alexandria.

[8] François Lanusse (1772–1801).

[9] Auguste Nicolas Baudot (1765–1801).

[10] Cesar Antoine Roize (1761–1801).

[11] John Hely Hutchinson, later Baron Hutchinson of Alexandria and Knocklofty, later still 2nd Early of Donoughmore (1757–1832).

The terms of the capitulation were generous. The French Army, at less than half its original strength, was repatriated in British ships without having to surrender its arms. Captain Moiret, regretting the loss of his Zulima, but, it would seem, resigned to anything could he only return to France, accounted himself lucky, as indeed he was, to bid farewell to the horrors of Egypt.

The surviving members of the Commission, after some discussion, retained their valuable documents, the fruit of three years of exhausting work. The artefacts they had collected were, however, confiscated by the British. Among these was the Rosetta Stone, but the French archaeologists retained wax impressions of this as well as of other similar valuable items, and in 1824 the Frenchman Champollion[12] beat his British rival in being the first to decipher the inscriptions of the Rosetta Stone.

It had been a bizarre episode. For France it had been damaging. Their disciplined, courageous and experienced army had been cruelly reduced. Officers of genius had been sacrificed. Generals Caffarelli du Falga of the Engineers, Dommartin[13] of the Artillery, Sulkowski,[14] Napoleon's aide-de-camp, and the brilliant Lanusse could ill be spared. Only Napoleon profited. His power was enhanced to the point that critical voices were to be silenced for years to come, and it was his account of the expedition that was remembered in France.

The only possible justification for the loss to France and the suffering endured by the army began to appear in 1802, when Napoleon ordered that work should begin on the publication of the 'Description of Egypt'. This monumental work comprised the artistic and scientific achievements of the Commission in ten folio volumes containing over eight hundred engravings and three thousand illustrations. Publication was completed in 1828 and it remains at once a memorial and a tribute to the members of the Commission who had not allowed their dedication to be undermined by disease, discomfort or danger. Thanks to their devotion to every aspect of Egyptian life and culture, Egyptian archaeology became a focus of interest in Europe and ultimately in North America. It was an interest which would have profound effects upon the subsequent development of the nation.

The departure of the French left memories of unfulfilled promises, glimpses of possible freedoms as well as ideas of democracy and the rule of law. The prospect of a revival of science and art persisted, as did a heightened national consciousness. Such a legacy of three years spent under French occupation was ineradicable, and slow to manifest itself.

---

[12] Jean François Champollion (1790–1832).

[13] Elzéar-Auguste Cousin de Dommartin (1768–1799).

[14] Jozef Sulkowski (1770[?]–1798) (see also Appendix 2).

Some aspects of the changes which had begun to take place were brutally reversed even as the last French transport sailed away.

The sad little story of Captain Moiret's love affair with the beautiful and unfortunate Zulima well illustrates the plight of women in that region and at that time. Egyptian authors have written of the effects of such a clash of cultures. The chronicler Al-Jabarti found the behaviour of women after the arrival of the French an intolerable scandal, and he was not alone in this view. Another writer, Niqūitā al-Turk, stated that 'The Muslims were horrified to see their wives and daughters appear with their faces unveiled in the company of the French. Death would have been preferable in their eyes.' [Amis de Malmaison] But, enchanted by the freedom and enjoyment now offered to them, many Muslim women adopted the manners of the French, wearing European dress, walking out in public with men and even taking part in business matters. At Damiette women were even allowed to use the public baths on one day a week. However, those who embraced the new liberty were to pay dearly for it – ancient customs are not so easily rejected. On their return to power in Egypt the Turks did not exact vengeance from the sheikhs who had shown friendship to the French, nor were the Copts who had enrolled in the French auxiliary units penalised, but the women who had discarded the strict Muslim conventions paid heavily. Al Jabarti describes the execution of two young girls of good family, accused of having unveiled and of wearing unseemly clothing. Such events caused panic, and the ancient morals and customs were quickly restored; it was to be more than a century before cautious steps in the direction of women's rights were to be taken.

Other movements towards change were stronger. The military incursion had provoked a brutal rupture with the past. The power of the Mameluks had been decisively broken; a long and arduous road had been opened which would lead at last to national independence. It was only after the departure of the French that Napoleon's promise to return the government of their country to the people began to become reality. There was far to go and it was under the ruthless guidance of Mohammed Ali,[15] a Turkish governor of Albanian extraction, that Egypt was Westernised and learned to look to Europe for technical guidance.

Select Bibliography

Al-Jabarti, *Napoleon in Egypt: Chronicle of the French Occupation 1798* (M. Wiener, Princeton, 1995)

---

[15] The Turkish Governor appears in many English language sources under the more common version of his name, Mehemet Ali.

Bourrienne, Louis Antoine Fauvelet de, *Memoirs of Napoleon Bonaparte* (Frederick A. Stokes, New York, 1903)

Cooper, Duff, *Tallyrand* (Harper, London, 1932)

Cronin, Vincent, *Napoleon Bonaparte* (Dell Publishing, New York, 1973)

Dhombres, Nicole, 'Napoléon et les Scientifiques, Part I: 1779–1798' in: *La Revue du Souvenir Napoléonien* **340** (1985), pp.2–26

Doguereau, Jean-Pierre, *Journal de l'Expédition d'Egypte* (Lavouivre, Paris, 1997)

Ghali, Ibrahim Amin, 'L'Expédition d'Egypte vue par les Auteurs Egyptiens' (Conference held by l'Assemblée Générale des Amis de Malmaison on 19 May 1976, and reproduced on the internet (www.napoleon.org) by kind permission of M. Gérard Hubert)

Herald, Christopher, *The Age of Napoleon* (Dell Publishing, New York, 1965)

Peterson, Robert K.D., 'Insects, Disease and Military History: The Napoleonic Campaigns and Historical Perception' in: *The American Entomologist* **41**: 3 (1995), pp.147–160

Pocock, Tom, A Thirst for Glory: The Life of Admiral Sir Sidney Smith (Aurum Press, London, 1996)

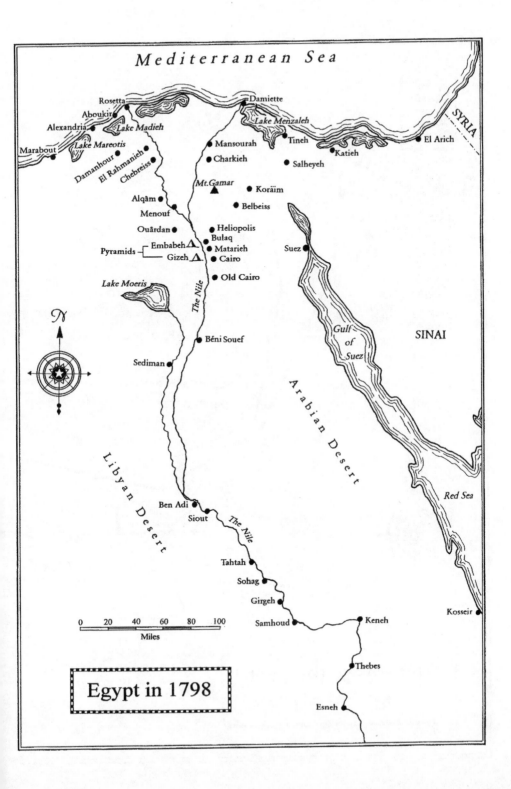

Mediterranean Sea

Rosetta
Aboukir
Alexandria
Marabout
Lake Madieh
Lake Mareotis
Damanhour
El Rahmanieh
Chebreiss

Damiette
Lake Menzaleh
Mansourah
Charkieh
Tineh
Katieh
Salheyeh
El Arich
SYRIA

Mt.Gamar
Koräim
Belbeiss

Alqâm
Menouf
Ouârdan
Pyramids—
Embabeh△
Gizeh △

Heliopolis
Bulaq
Matarieh
Cairo
Old Cairo

Suez

Lake Moeris

The Nile

Béni Souef

Sediman

Gulf of Suez

SINAI

Arabian Desert

N

Libyan Desert

Ben Adi
Siout
The Nile

Tahtah
Sohag
Girgeh
Samhoud
Keneh

Red Sea

Kosseir

Thebes

Esneh

0   20   40   60   80   100
Miles

Egypt in 1798

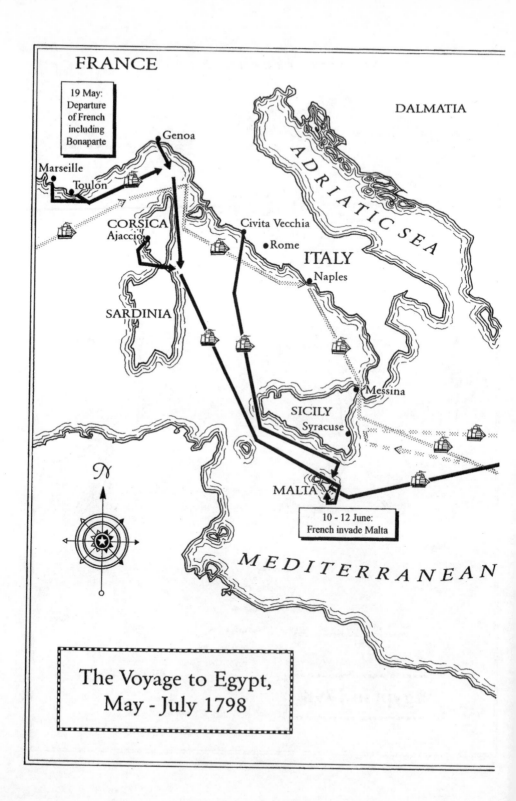

FRANCE

19 May:
Departure
of French
including
Bonaparte

Genoa

DALMATIA

Marseille
Toulon

A D R I A T I C   S E A

CORSICA
Ajaccio

Civita Vecchia

Rome

ITALY

Naples

SARDINIA

Messina

SICILY
Syracuse

MALTA

10 - 12 June:
French invade Malta

N

M E D I T E R R A N E A N

The Voyage to Egypt,
May - July 1798

BLACK SEA

OTTOMAN EMPIRE

GREECE

ANATOLIA

MOREA

Korone

CYPRUS

1 August:
French fleet
discovered
and destroyed
at Aboukir Bay
by returning
British

CRETE

SEA

Aboukir

Alexandria

1 July:
Marabout landings begin

28 June:
Premature arrival of
British results in their
failure to intercept
French landings.
Nelson continues
pursuit

French

British

0   100   200   300

Miles

EGYPT

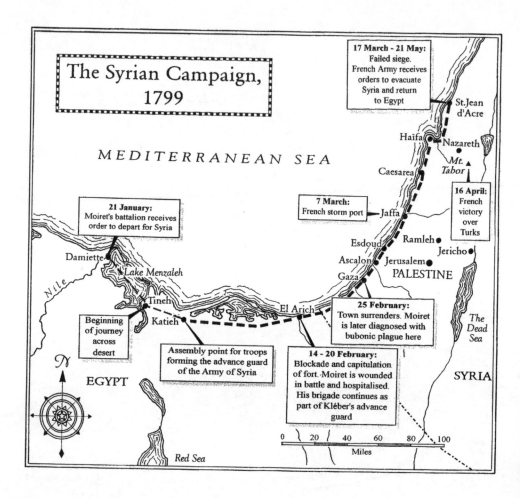

The Syrian Campaign, 1799

MEDITERRANEAN SEA

17 March - 21 May:
Failed siege.
French Army receives
orders to evacuate
Syria and return
to Egypt

St.Jean
d'Acre

Haifa   Nazareth

Caesarea   Mt.
               Tabor

7 March:
French storm port   Jaffa

16 April:
French
victory
over
Turks

21 January:
Moiret's battalion receives
order to depart for Syria

Damiette

Lake Menzaleh

Nile

Tineh

Beginning
of journey
across
desert

Katieh

Esdoud   Ramleh

Ascalon   Jerusalem   Jericho

Gaza   PALESTINE

El Arich

25 February:
Town surrenders. Moiret
is later diagnosed with
bubonic plague here

The
Dead
Sea

Assembly point for troops
forming the advance guard
of the Army of Syria

14 - 20 February:
Blockade and capitulation
of fort. Moiret is wounded
in battle and hospitalised.
His brigade continues as
part of Kléber's advance
guard

SYRIA

EGYPT

N

0   20   40   60   80   100
              Miles

Red Sea

THE MEMOIRS

CHAPTER I

THE DEPARTURE FROM TOULON – BONAPARTE'S FIRST PROCLAMATION –
THE INVASION OF MALTA – IMPRESSIONS OF THE MALTESE – THE TAK-
ING OF ALEXANDRIA – BONAPARTE ADDRESSES THE EGYPTIAN PEOPLE

In the month of Floréal, Year VI [May 1798], troops totalling about twenty
thousand, and consisting of equal numbers of infantry, cavalry and artillery,
were mustered in and around Toulon. A fleet of thirteen ships of the line
rode at anchor in the port, together with seventeen frigates, several brigs,
corvettes, gunships and barges, as well as a number of other merchantmen,
all awaiting the assembly of the army. At the same time, additional transport
vessels were being prepared at Bastia in Corsica and at Civita Vecchia,
which were destined to join up with the squadron at Toulon.

The union of all these forces gave the expedition a total of thirty thousand combatants, not counting the sailors, ships masters, scholars, artists
and administrative officials or the officers. Such preparations, coming at a
time when the invasion of England was being talked about, were bound to
cause endless speculation amongst the soldiers, each of whom felt himself to
be sufficiently shrewd and well-informed to divine the goal of the expedition. Some said that they were about to seize Sardinia, others thought that
the objectives were to be Sicily and Malta in order to gain an empire in the
Mediterranean for the Republic and to humble the British flag. Some were
convinced that the aim was to pass through the Straits of Gibraltar, lift the
blockade of Cadiz, join up with the Spanish squadron and our fleet in Brest,
and then accomplish the invasion of England. Others were sure that Egypt
was the destination and, from there, to continue on to the East Indies, in
order to destroy the English settlements and ruin their trade. The clever
young men, known to us as the Scholars, as well as the artists, were almost
all of the latter view. Such then were the uncertainties which divided
opinion and troubled minds. Their concern was the greater as all were
sincerely devoted to the glory and the well-being of their native land.

Meanwhile, the army, charged with achieving these aims for France,

35

maintained its usual calm. The men, having complete confidence in their general, never had the slightest doubt of ultimate success, no matter what the undertaking might prove to be. Bonaparte had guaranteed it and his word was enough. As soon as we were embarked, but before we left the anchorage, we received the following proclamation from him:

From Toulon 21st Floréal of the Year VI of the Republic [10th May 1798]
Bonaparte, Commanding General of the Army, to the soldiers and the sailors of the Mediterranean

Soldiers,
You are one of the divisions of the Army of England: you have waged war in the mountains and on the plains, you have laid siege to cities. Now the time has come to fight on the sea.

The Roman legions, which you have sometimes resembled but not yet equalled, fought the might of Carthage on this same sea and on the plains of Zama. Victory was always theirs, for they were ever brave, patient and unmindful of fatigue; they were disciplined and united in their aim.

Soldiers, the eyes of Europe are on you! You have a great destiny to fulfil, battles to win, dangers and difficulties to overcome. You will achieve even more than ever before for the prosperity of the fatherland, the welfare of mankind and your own glory.

Soldiers, sailors, infantry, cavalry and artillery, be as one! Always remember that on the battlefield you need each other. Soldiers and sailors, you have, until now, been neglected; today you are the first concern of the Republic: you will be worthy of the Army of which you are part.

The spirit of liberty has, since its birth, made the Republic the arbiter of Europe; pray that it may ever be so across the seas and in the most distant countries.
Bonaparte.

Shouts of approval and the singing of patriotic songs resounded from the ships following the reading of this oration. The favourable wind for which we waited soon arose, and the fleet sailed, at last, on 29th and 30th Floréal, Year VI of the Republic [18th and 19th May 1798].

I was with a light squadron composed of the ships *Franklin*, *Aquilon*, *Spartiate* and some frigates. We weighed anchor first and sailed to wait near the Hyères islands, where the fleet was to join up. This took place on the following day, having been a little delayed by a contrary wind. The pilots were soon ready and we set sail. Our circuitous route concealed our objective and baffled the speculations of the sailors. Do we follow the coast? It is so that we may disembark at Genoa. Do we leave the coast? It is to go to Sardinia. The predictions varied from minute to minute. The uncertainty seemed at an end when the order was received to hasten towards Sardinia. 'Ah! This is it', they said, 'We disembark tonight and tomorrow we shall be masters of the island.' But to the surprise of these prophets, after spending a few days lying off the coast the order was received to make for the open sea. Once more we were out of sight of land. 'Now, there is no question about it', declared the marine officers, whose opinions were always listened to, 'We're off to Sicily!' Then it was heard that English sails had been sighted; this rumour, which was spread furtively, led us to fear that the Civita Vecchia convoy, which should have joined us off Sardinia, might have fallen victim to the enemy. This apprehension grew stronger when several sails were sighted in the distance. Our squadron was ordered to pursue them. The *Spartiate* set off and recognised the sails as those of some of our own group which had been separated from us by a strong gust of wind. But the uncertainty remained and fear increased. Soon we lay off Sicily. The speed with which we skirted the coast disabused the sailors of their impression that we should disembark on that island. 'Now it is quite certain', they said, 'We are heading for Malta.' This time, perhaps, they have guessed correctly. We shall see.

As we drifted at the whim of the winds and of Neptune, we again saw distant ships which did not appear to be French. This must be the advance guard of the English! The Admiral ordered an investigation. The *Spartiate* set off and found four Danish ships laden with grain for Malta. We arrested them and this action seemed to us proof that Malta was our goal. We discussed this thoroughly and no one could doubt any longer the truth of our conjecture.

The winds were still favourable as we approached this celebrated island and we looked on it as the Promised Land – the end of our journey. Just then we saw many ships. Some said that this was the English squadron while others assured us that the vessels were French. Our minds were soon put at rest as we recognised the *Courageuse* escorting the convoy from Civita Vecchia, which we had been concerned about ever since we sailed.

It had reached us in good order after all, not having suffered any attacks or damage; we were overjoyed. The English were in the Mediterranean in strength and we were delighted not to have met them. 'Destiny is on our side!' the General said. He was right, and the army were of the same mind when we arrived off the island on the evening of the 21st Prairial [9th June 1798]. Advantage was taken of the darkness to land some troops on the beach and the rest of the disembarkation took place on the following day. The Maltese prepared to defend themselves and rained bombs, bullets and grape-shot on us. This hailstorm did not surprise or dampen the enthusiasm of our soldiers who, protected by the ships' gunboats, crossed the beach, leapt into the fortifications and slew or took prisoner all who opposed them.

The enemy retreated and took up new positions in which to await new

37

defeats. The French, used to striking whilst the iron was hot, and not content with the laurels they had gained, set off in pursuit as usual. With their bayonets in their enemies' backs they gained victory after victory. The battle lasted twenty-four hours and the Maltese surrendered. The Knights abandoned the Cross and handed over the town and the island of Malta. (The town is called Cité-Valette.[16])

We entered the city on the 24th Prairial, Year VI [12th June 1798], and the squadron sailed into the port on the following day, the 25th. We were not a little astonished to find ourselves masters of a city protected by its position on the edge of the sea, surrounded by impenetrable fortifications, bristling with cannons and flanked on all sides by formidable towers.[17] It is true, however, that the defenders were indifferent soldiers and they were not commanded by a Grand Master like la Valette.[18] It is certain that, defended by the French, only famine or treason could have led to defeat. The Grand Master of the Order of Malta who capitulated to us was Baron de Hompesch. He was promised a pension of three hundred thousand francs by the French Republic, and pensions of seven hundred francs for those of the Knights who had been born in France, until such time as their fate should be decided at the Congress of Rastadt.

The character of the Maltese people made us aware that we were no longer at the civilised heart of Europe. Sombre, melancholy and sullen, avoiding our glances and our company, we were made to feel their dislike. All the houses were shuttered and the roads deserted, which was evidence of the universal wretchedness and desolation. What an appalling country! I thought then that there was no more horrible place in the world, but it will be seen later how wrong I was!

The women, black veiled, proclaimed only their misery and gave rise to no thoughts other than contempt or at least disdain. In this famous island we found only laurels without myrtle; the French find it almost impossible to separate the two. We turned our hopes towards Egypt; our imagination, inflamed by our memory of history, endowed each Egyptian lady with the charms of a Cleopatra. Our arrival and our stay in Egypt certainly made us reconsider our fond illusions, and we often thought with regret of the banks of the Po, the Tiber, the Rhine and the Oder. How many times did we curse

---

[16] The capital of Malta, in the centre of the island, was then called Cité-Notable.
[17] Napoleon had sent his agents ahead to bribe those knights who held Republican beliefs and to foment ill-feeling against the Grand Master, who was of German descent.
[18] Jean Parisot de la Valette (1494–1568), Grand Master of the Order of the Knights of St John of Jerusalem, defended Malta against the Turks. He has been described as the greatest Grand Master in the history of the Order.

the lying descriptions of the author of *Letters From Egypt*! But let us get back to our story.

As soon as arrangements had been made in Malta to implement the plans of our Commander-in-Chief, a garrison was left there consisting of three or four thousand men under the command of General Vaubois,[19] and the rest of us set sail on 29th Prairial [17th June 1798].

During our voyage we occupied ourselves once more with the same speculations, the same discussions as those we had had between Toulon and Malta. 'We're going back to Sicily', said some. 'Certainly not', responded others, 'From the way we're going, it's clear we are heading straight to Candie.'[20]

'You are quite wrong', said others, 'We are heading for Egypt', and this was the most popular opinion, and the best founded.

The Commander-in-Chief put an end to argument and speculation by issuing the following proclamation:

From Headquarters, Near-East, 14th Messidor in Year VI of the Republic [2nd July 1798]
Bonaparte, member of the National Institute, Commanding General

Soldiers,
You are about to attempt a conquest, the effects of which will be immeasurable both for civilisation and for world commerce. You will deal a cruel blow to England where it will be most felt, even as you prepare to deal the mortal stroke.

We shall undertake weary marches and fight many battles; we shall succeed in everything. Destiny is on our side.

The Mameluk Beys,[21] who favour English trade exclusively, have insulted our merchants and tyrannised the miserable inhabitants of the Nile. A few days after our arrival they will cease to exist.

The people amongst whom we shall live are Mohammedans. Their chief article of faith is this: Allah is Allah and Mohammed is his Prophet. Never argue with this. Behave towards them as you have towards the Jews and the Italians. Show the same respect for their Muftis and their Imams as you have shown towards Rabbis and Bishops. The same tolerance must be shown to their ceremonies, which are governed by the Koran, and to their mosques, as you have displayed to convents and synagogues, and to the religion of Moses and Jesus Christ.

The Roman legions protected all faiths. You will find here many customs different from those of Europe, and you must learn to accept them. The people we are among treat their women differently from us, but in every land

---

[19] Charles Henri Vaubois (1748–1839), Count from 1808.
[20] Candie was then a port in Crete.
[21] The Mameluk Beys were a warrior caste who held power in Egypt.

those who rape are monsters. Plunder enriches only a few, but it dishonours us all and weakens us; it makes enemies of those people we need to have as friends.

The first town we shall enter was built by Alexander. Everywhere we shall see great reminders of the past, worthy of our emulation.
Bonaparte.

This proclamation convinced us that our destination was Egypt, and all our hopes were now fixed on the success of this brilliant and glorious enterprise. We were now to set our eyes on this ancient land, cradle of science and the arts! We were delighted! We should explore the valleys where the children of Israel had tended their flocks, and rediscover the eternal monuments built by the power of the Pharaohs. We should see the pyramids, the obelisks, the ruins of old temples, the towns and the land made famous by the exploits of Macedonians, Romans, Mohammedans and the saintliest of our own kings! Enough to excite the thoughts and fire the courage of a French officer with any knowledge of the past! We could not wait to set our feet on the dust so often trodden by the Macedonian phalanxes, by the Roman legions and the blessed battalions of the Crusaders. We burned to surpass the pagan heroes and to avenge the spilled blood of our Christian forefathers. We flattered ourselves that we should restore civilisation with the rule of science and art, and give a new birth to abundance, fruitfulness and happiness. This new colony would compensate for the loss of those torn from us by the crafty English in the New World.

Who can express the delightful illusions with which we flattered ourselves and which were the subject of most of our conversations at this time. The very wind seemed in tune with our wishes, and we were driven quickly toward the town which owed its name and its existence to the vanquisher of Darius. We could already see its towers and minarets. Our General ordered one of the frigates away to reconnoitre: the frigate sighted an Egyptian vessel and boarded her, forcing the Egyptian ship, after the usual formalities, to lead the way to their flag ship. The commander of this vessel, having no option but to obey, came to us and informed us that two days earlier the English fleet had appeared off Alexandria. We felt renewed fear, 'suppose our disembarkation was to be opposed by a superior force!' And there, once more, were the English sails! Oh! this time we should surely encounter a stubborn, perhaps deadly, resistance. 'Fortune, have you forsaken me?', cried Bonaparte, 'Grant me just five more days!'

We continued on our way resolutely, and arrived off the coast of Egypt without opposition. The vessel which had been sighted and which had caused all our alarm proved to be a French boat called the *Justice*, which had been to contact our Consul in Alexandria and was coming to rejoin our fleet. During the night we placed several gunboats along the coast off

Alexandria. Under the protection of these boats, detachments of the various corps completed their disembarkation, despite the efforts of Egyptian troops and a group of Alexandrians. These troops, called Mameluks,[22] were cavalry, paid by and in the service of the Beys. All were mounted on horses fleeter than the wind, and were invariably armed with a carbine, a pair of pistols and a finely tempered Damascus sabre. These horsemen were invincible by any other troops of the same type. Our own, good though they were, could not be compared with them because of the superiority of their mounts.

The generals Bon,[23] Kléber and Menou divided between them the advance guard of thirteen hundred men and went forward without cannon or cavalry towards Alexandria, while the rest of the army continued to disembark and the artillery made ready to leave. The first shots were fired by three hundred Arab horsemen who had been guarding the heights around the town and who retreated precipitately when they saw the three divisions which composed our advance guard. Bonaparte, arriving at the walls of the Arab town (otherwise known as the Old Town), prepared to begin negotiations, but batteries were all at once disclosed which poured shot upon our soldiers, who were thus reduced to the necessity of winning a victory. To their grape-shot we returned a lively fusillade which caused the mob of peasants, behind which the Mameluks concealed themselves, to bite the dust. Fire from our gunboats also came to our assistance and the enemy soon fled. They rallied a short distance away and joined up with some newly arrived troops. This reinforcement gave them confidence and they attacked once more. On our side, the advance guard was receiving continual reinforcements and stood firm against an enemy which, by reason of the speed of its horses, many thought invincible. The enemy charged a second time and enjoyed even less success. They retreated, and again tried several times, in vain, to break through our battalions, whose numbers continued to be increased at many points. Finally we captured the village under attack, despite the resistance of the Mameluks and their slaves. Some of us scaled the walls and others broke down the gates. Then we bivouacked, some outside the village and the rest within; the general staff occupied the houses of the most important citizens.

Our entry into Alexandria took place on 15th Messidor Year VI [3rd July 1798]. The English had spread terror amongst the inhabitants prior to our

---

[22] Mameluks: literally 'bought men', mercenaries. Originally brought from the Caucasus as young slaves, their Beys now virtually ruled Egypt, collecting revenues from which they paid a small amount to the Pasha in Cairo, who sent it to the Sultan in Constantinople as a tribute (see Short Biographies).

[23] Louis André Bon (1758–1799).

arrival, depicting us as bloody savages and rapists, devoid of all decency, so the Alexandrians anticipated that we should wreak a terrible vengeance on them for having resisted us, a vengeance which they felt they merited only too well. All this led them to fear that their town, taken by force, would be put to fire and the sword in accordance with practice in war.

Imagine their surprise – even their admiration – to see shining in us that moderation, that gentle humanity which we had so often shown in other countries. Their fears were soothed; they found that we had respect for their religion, where they had been led to believe that we had none. The security we offered to them and to their property helped to reassure these misguided and frightened people, especially when they had heard the following proclamation by our General-in-Chief.

Alexandria, 15th Messidor in Year VI of the Republic [3rd July 1798]
Bonaparte, Member of the National Institute, General-in-Chief

To the Egyptian people,
For many years the Beys who govern Egypt have insulted the French nation, and humiliated our merchants. The hour of their punishment has arrived. For very many years a mob of slaves, bought in the Caucasus and in Georgia, have tyrannised the loveliest part of the world, but God, who governs everything, has decreed that their rule is ended.

People of Egypt, they will tell you that I come here to destroy your religion, do not believe them; reply that I have come to restore your rights, to punish the usurpers and that, far more than the Mameluks, I respect God, His Prophet, Mohammed and the Holy Koran. Tell them that, before God, all men are equal. Wisdom, ability and virtue are the only differences between them. But what wisdom, what virtues, what talents, distinguish the Mameluks to entitle them to own everything that makes life comfortable and happy? Is there fertile land? It belongs to the Mameluks; a handsome slave, a fine horse, a noble house? They all belong to the Mameluks.

If Egypt is their farm, let them show the lease they have signed with God. But God is just and merciful to the people.

All Egyptians are now called upon to manage everything. The cleverest, the wisest and the most virtuous will govern and the people will be happy. There used to be great towns, broad canals and rich trade in this land. What destroyed them if it was not the greed, the injustice and the tyranny of the Mameluks?

Caliphs, Sheikhs, Imams, tell the people that we are the friends of true Muslims. Did we not overthrow the Pope and the Knights of Malta because these enemies believed that God wished them to wage war against Muslims? Is it not we, who, throughout the centuries, have fought on the side of the Sultan (may God grant his wishes!) and for the enemies of his enemies? Have not the Mameluks, on the other hand, consistently opposed the authority of the Sultan whom they still do not acknowledge? They recognise only their own whims. Thrice blessed are those who are with us! They will prosper both in wealth and rank. Happy are those who are neutral! They will be granted the time to learn to know us, and will come over to our side. But woe, triple woe, to those who take up arms with the Mameluks and fight against us. There will be no hope for them, they will perish!

1st Item.
All villages within a radius of three miles of the route taken by the Army are required to send a deputation to inform the commanding generals of the troops that they are submissive and inform them that they wish to fly the flag of the French Army.

2nd Item.
All villages which take up arms against the French Army will be burned.

3rd Item.
All the villages subjugated by the Army will display, together with the Sultan's flag, that of the Army.

4th Item.
The sheikhs will cause seals to be affixed to the goods, the houses, shops and other properties of the Mameluks. They will be careful that nothing is misappropriated.

5th Item.
The sheikhs, imams and caliphs will continue to perform their usual duties. All persons are to remain at home, prayers will take place as usual. Everyone must thank God for the destruction of the Mameluks and cry 'Glory to the Sultan! Glory to the French Army which is his friend. Curses on the heads of the Mameluks! Happiness to the Egyptian people!'
Bonaparte.

This proclamation produced an immediate and beneficial effect. It dispelled the people's suspicion of us and they showed us more friendliness, some even offering their help. The ports were now occupied by the ships of the convoy. The vessels of the squadron now lay at anchor in Aboukir Bay to complete the landing of the artillery. The forts by the lighthouse were manned by companies of grenadiers.

Those Bedouins who in the morning had opposed our advance guard now sent a deputation of thirty men to offer our General the bread of peace. To demonstrate the honesty of his intentions the French General ate it and gave them presents. The Arabs returned home, filled with gratitude which, however, did not prevent them from robbing all the French people they met on their way.

CHAPTER II

THE BEDOUINS AND THE ALEXANDRIANS – JOURNEY TO ROSETTA – ARRIVAL AT EL RAHMANIEH – THE BATTLE OF CHEBREISS – ADVANCE ON CAIRO

Before going further it might be as well to give the reader some idea of the Egyptian people. It is thought that the Bedouins were the original rulers of the country from which they were expelled by the Mameluks, just as the Mameluks have been by us. They always lived in the desert in tents. Their leaders were the Emirs, and under them were the sheikhs; they claimed to be descended from Ishmael, the son of Abraham and Agar. Their only occupations were those of thieves, assassins and brigands. Unhappy the traveller who, defenceless, falls into their hands! The Bedouins speed hither and thither upon their superb Arab horses – similar to those favoured by the Mameluks. They are utterly depraved. Something which appeared to me strange, not to say extraordinary, is the fact that each mounted Bedouin, armed with carbine, two pistols and a damascene sabre, is always accompanied by a young slave, who runs with the horse, holding onto the stirrup with one hand. No matter how fast the horse, the slave never lets go.

As for the Alexandrians, who were the first Africans I studied, here is the picture I formed of them. The men were usually of a sturdy constitution, swarthy, and many of them very black or mulatto. Their clothes consisted only of a few rags thrown on anyhow; on their heads they wore cloths twisted into a bird's nest shape, which they called turbans. They wore neither stockings nor shoes. Others were as nature made them and left nature's works on view. Such were the lower orders in Egypt. They were nothing but tenant-farmers for the Mameluks, who owned everything – houses, land and buildings – and who exacted a large annual rent.

The clothing of the rich differed from that of the poor only in the delicacy and beauty of the fabric. Over a costly silken shirt was worn a sort of habit, like those of the former monks in France, but of enormous value;

44

they wore breeches of an amplitude that would require ten or twelve yards of cloth to make, and for shoes there were magnificent slippers of Morocco leather. Their turbans, must, by reason of their opulence, have been extremely expensive. Their hair was shaved except for a small patch at the top of their heads. It was by that bit of hair, they said, that the Prophet Mohammed would, at their last breath, come and seize them to raise them to Paradise. Their beards were allowed to grow and were never cut.

The women were dressed in a long blue cotton gown which covered only part of their nakedness; the bosom was always on view to everyone. Their faces, however, were a different matter; they were carefully covered up with a black veil wound round the neck and matching another veil draped over the head, to which it was attached by hooks. This left only the eyes visible and looked, in a way, like the helmets with visors which were worn by our valiant knights, about to break a lance in tournament. Their gowns were often so inadequate as to display that which merited concealment far more than their faces. They went bare-foot like the men and like them were of a swarthy complexion. In all the villages it was usual to see girls of twelve to fourteen years old going about naked. Misery had brought them to this indecency which so shocked our morals and our customs.

The houses in this country are earth hovels of a matchless squalor. The people have no furniture or utensils other than earthenware pots and wooden bowls and spoons. Cupboards are unknown to them because they have no wood and no carpenters. Their food consists of a little goat's milk and a few bits of dough cooked in the sun. The corn, which is shared, for it is harvested twice a year, is not made good use of except in the towns. They know nothing of windmills. Mohammed, whose laws are obeyed, forbids the use of wine, so they drink only water and, occasionally, for a special treat, a sort of beverage made from the juice of the palm, which tastes somewhat like our liquorice water.

Such are the customs in the country, and even in the towns. The latter have roads, usually shaded by sloping roofs of reeds or flax straw.

The Egyptian manner of eating seemed to me no less strange than everything else. Their tables are large round pieces of leather, spread on a mat on the ground. The more important men sit around this, their legs crossed like tailors, while their inferiors kneel or squat on their heels. Forks are never used; it is actually a sign of devoutness not to use a fork. They maintain that Mohammed had shown mercy to those who ate with the three fingers of one hand; therefore, they seize all food with their fingers, always of the right hand, because the left is used for washing after bodily functions. As the meat was cut up and well cooked, pieces were easy to pick up. Knives were not provided either. The soup, the broth, the roast, the stews, the desserts, the salads and the fruits were all served at the same time.

45

There was nothing to drink except when extreme need forced a request for, at least, a drink of water. When the meal was finished all rose and gave thanks to God. A drink was taken and then the hands were washed with soap; finally there was coffee and pipes were smoked.

The lower orders ate even more messily; they grabbed from huge wooden bowls a handful of the rice, meat and pilau put before them. This they pressed in their palms into a sort of ball which they then crammed whole into their mouths. If any was left clinging to their hands or to their beards, they shook or scraped it back into the bowl. As they ate they took great gulps from a jug of water that was passed from one to another and, after having cleaned their hands with earth in the absence of soap, they too took coffee.

This pilau was the most popular sort of stew and consisted only of rice which had been boiled for a short time in water, or in a meat broth with saffron, raisins, peas and onions, until it was half cooked. It was then taken off the heat and left covered near the fire to swell up. Melted butter with pepper and sometimes sugar was then added. Rice was also added to soup, which was usually made with chopped up pieces of sheep, goat and chicken.

This, then, is what our soldiers called *ratatouille* – not very attractive, as can be seen.

Ancient writers have spoken of the Psylles or eaters of serpents, and modern travellers have claimed that some of them still exist in Egypt. As for me, I have seen men with snakes as thick as their legs making them do different tricks and teaching them to wind around their bodies without doing them the least harm. They could be likened to the men with dancing bears in France. But I have never seen any of them eat snakes and tear them with their teeth.

No ploughing is done in Egypt. When the Nile recedes and the ground is still damp, the seed is sown on the silt and the grain grows with no further care.

I will leave it to the reader to decide whether, in comparison with such a country, Malta was not a more attractive place, in spite of some horrors we had found there. He may find it easy to believe that Alexandria, where we had hoped to find such fine sights and so many pleasures, and where we found only the hideous spectacle of misery, ugliness and squalor, caused us bitterly to miss the charms of home and to long passionately for our return to Europe. Alas! We were fallen between Scylla and Charybdis. The women whom we had found so horrible in Malta now appeared to us to be veritable Venuses compared to those of Alexandria. As much as we had distained them we now desired them. How terribly the subjects and fellow country-women of the beautiful Cleopatra had degenerated, we thought. Should we not fear a series of even more horrible events if things continued to deteriorate like this? Our happiness certainly did not match our success!

Nothing remained of Alexandria's ancient monuments except Pompey's column in the middle and the two obelisks of Cleopatra, one still standing and the other fallen to the ground. I sat on the fallen one, and then walked along its length. I was rather like a dwarf, who, having felled a giant, took pleasure in trampling him underfoot. What a symbol of the fate of human grandeur. Pompey's column looked very much like the one in the Place Vendôme in Paris except that its capital was of the Corinthian style and its shaft a single block. M. Dolomieu,[24] a member of the Egyptian Institute, thought that the date of erection of this column should have been placed in the period following the reign of Constantine, because the capital and the pedestal bore, in his view, the signs of degradation characteristic of that era, whereas the shaft was of an earlier date when the skills involved were practised in all their purity.

The standing obelisk marked the place where the palace of Cleopatra once stood. There it was that the queen, celebrated for her beauty, her skills and her wiles, snared Anthony in her toils, chained his tireless energy, cradled him in her voluptuous breast and enticed him to journey with her on the Nile, instead of setting sail for Rome, which then, because of his weakness, closed her gates to him forever. Near to these columns, the proud Queen of Egypt, seated on a golden throne, received in the eyes of the world the title of wife of Anthony, who sacrificed his glory to her. Having lost the chance of victory as she indulged in these pleasures she caused herself to be bitten by an asp; he fell on his sword, their death providing posterity with a striking instance of the dreadful consequences of infatuation.

We were now masters of the important island of Malta and of the town of Alexandria, which consisted only of the remains of a city once flourishing and illustrious, and a depraved people who had been brutalised and enslaved. We soon saw that we could never civilise them or restore them to their former glory. This latest conquest seemed hardly worth the few men it had cost us. We had sustained a hundred wounded, and we had lost, amongst others M. Masse the Brigade-Major, as well as some other officers, non-commissioned officers and men. Generals Kléber and Menou and Staff-Colonel Lescalle were also wounded more or less seriously.

On 17th Messidor [5th July 1798] the army set off in pursuit of the Mameluks. It marched in three columns, one on the right, another in the centre headed towards Damanhour, the third on the left marching close to the sea in the direction of Rosetta. I was with this third column, so I had no

---

[24] Dieudonné Dolomieu, a geologist and member of the Scientific Commission which accompanied the expedition (see also Appendix 2).

first hand knowledge of what happened to the other two columns until our eventual reunion; all I know is that they were harassed daily during their march by the Bedouin Arabs, who spared none who fell back to the end of the column through sickness or exhaustion. They also, like ourselves, suffered much from heat, thirst and lack of food. Although a peace treaty had been signed with the Bedouin Arabs, yet, as I noted above, it must be admitted that this would not have become known as soon as it was signed and it would have taken time for the news to have spread. For this reason certain tribes, unaware of the treaty or its contents, continued to practise their banditry on us as much as on the Mameluks whenever the occasion presented itself.

Our division, which was Kléber's, commanded by General Dugua,[25] left Alexandria on 6th July for the purpose of seizing Rosetta, a town on the west tributary of the Nile at one of the angles of the delta. We were barely two hours from Alexandria when we found ourselves plunged into the desert sands, where we at once suffered torments of weariness and thirst. We marched all day without ever encountering a habitation or any fresh water with which to quench our thirst. We were exposed to the blazing sun and burned beneath the fiery sky. Several of our companions had learned from travellers that fresh water springs might be found near to the sea. We dug into the earth but found nothing there but a little brackish water which was insufficient for our needs. Several soldiers died of thirst, and others of drinking immoderately and without restraint of this salty water. We found no sweet water until we were approaching the outskirts of Aboukir. We made camp near this little town and left on the following morning, when we had to cross the small inlet of the sea which separated Alexandrian territory from that of Rosetta.

This day was not so exhausting as the first as we were obliged to wait for the small boats which were to ferry us across, which had not yet arrived. When we had crossed, we camped a mile further on, leaving again at 3 o'clock in the morning. In the course of this day we suffered the worst pangs that thirst and heat could provide, so that when we arrived at Rosetta most of us were staggering with fatigue, and we devoured everything refreshing we could find – water, grapes and dates. The Jews sold us a few bottles of bad wine at a very high price. Rosetta which, after having spent a few months elsewhere in Egypt, seemed quite an attractive town and very pleasant, only served to confirm us in the bad opinion which we had formed of the country.

Rosetta was built in a primitive style like all the other Egyptian towns. It did not deserve the name it bore – Rose of Egypt – except through the value

---

[25] Charles François Joseph Dugua (1744–1802).

of the commerce which it enjoyed with neighbouring countries, and with Europe by way of the Mediterranean and the Nile Delta; but none of these advantages had influenced in the slightest the morals and behaviour of the inhabitants which differed not at all from those I have already described.

We remained at Rosetta on the 21st Messidor [9th July] and departed at midnight. During the day we gathered stocks of biscuits and other necessaries for the journey, and we endured many fewer discomforts than we had experienced previously. Also the Nile, which we followed, provided us with fresh water, the want of which had caused us such suffering before; the land on the banks of the river, being well-watered, supplied us with more provisions than the desert we had just travelled across.

On the 22nd we bivouacked at the riverside about five miles from Rosetta, leaving on the following day for El Rahmanieh, where we rejoined the other two columns of the Army.

On the 24th the Commanding General held a review of the entire Army, giving rise to the hope that there would be a prompt return to France followed by an invasion of England. This prospect helped us to forget the troubles and weariness we had already experienced in Egypt and gave us the resignation to face those we had yet to meet.

We had hardly arrived at El Rahmanieh before the Mameluks began again to challenge us with frequent limited attacks. Many times the 15th Regiment of Dragoons attempted to charge them, but the fleetness of their horses carried them out of reach of our sabres.

On the same day several Egyptian boats, filled with provisions for Cairo, appeared level with our camp on their way upstream. They were stopped by our flotilla which forced them back, for we had gunboats and brigs armed with artillery on the Nile. As they retired downstream the Egyptian boats were met by other French vessels which attempted to make them surrender or fight. But the Egyptians made a pretence of surrendering by striking their flag while at the same time trying to slip away. When their trickery was perceived several rounds were fired at them, but it was too late, they had already escaped us.

For several days the rumour had been going around that the Mameluks, having learned in Cairo of our disembarkation, had rounded up and were about to cut the throats of all the European residents of the town. This news had the effect of speeding up our march.

On the 24th we left El Rahmanieh, and on the 25th were approaching Chebreiss when we saw that the Mameluks, sheltering behind their earthworks, were preparing to give battle.

We then made ready to give them a warm welcome. The Commanding General formed our divisions into squares and ordered them to advance in echelon. The enemy attempted several cavalry charges but without any success; then he turned and swerved, attempting to find a gap in our ranks. Finally he thought he had found one, between the Nile and the Army. Proud of his discovery he attacked there, rashly. But this had been anticipated. The enemy had hardly advanced more than a few paces when he received, almost point blank, a burst of musket fire from a French detachment which was lying in ambush. Many enemy cavalrymen were hit and fell dead from their horses onto the bloody sand. Others fled and sought the protection of eight or ten gunboats moored in the river and the batteries positioned on the bank. But our flotilla struck back with cannon fire. The gunboats of Murad Bey replied and the battle continued on the water.

The battle, undecided for a long time, looked likely to favour the enemy fleet, which was about to seize the strongest of our brigs, when suddenly our ships approached and boldly proceeded to board the enemy, fighting off all opposition. Other troops advanced on the batteries on the bank and carried off the cannons. Having attempted several ineffectual charges, the enemy decided to engage in a mass attack: his cavalry swung round and fell upon us with the speed of lightning. We allowed them to approach to a certain distance before our field pieces thundered, overwhelming the attackers with fire and shot. The carnage caused was so terrible that the survivors did not wait for the ensuing volleys which, nevertheless, rendered their rout complete. Their precipitate flight soon placed them beyond the reach of our bullets and cannonballs. This victory was due to the army's unruffled and perfect discipline. Lacking food, and even more important, drink, the soldier learned to be patient and to endure and to display the indisputable courage he had so often shown. This triumph was made even more pleasant as the troops could now hope for an improvement in their prospects. Mindful of this, the General caused the army to march along the Nile so that it was within reach of water. It was more difficult to obtain supplies of bread, which was extremely scarce among us. Egyptian peasants ate little of it, or actually did not know how to make it. We had nothing to eat but some rotten beans and occasionally rotten buffalo meat, though horse-meat was sometimes provided instead.

It was with these scanty resources that we marched on the 26th, 27th and 28th without meeting any enemies except the Bedouin Arabs who followed us, like sharks following ships at sea, to murder and rob any stragglers. They even swooped on the flanks, threatening a similar fate to anyone who strayed too far from the main body of the army. It can easily be seen that the difficulties which had beset us for so long were bound to result in disorder and pilfering, which even the care of the officers could not always prevent. As a consequence the officers had a much harder time of it than the ordinary soldiers, who managed to obtain food by pillage and violence. This in turn made it impossible for the officers to buy food and tact prevented us from sharing meals with our subordinates. So, while the soldiers feasted on pigeons, poultry and other stolen goods, the officers were reduced, for many days, to eating only a disgusting and inadequate portion of beans. We had never, anywhere, experienced such hunger and weariness: there were forced marches under the burning sun, lack of wine, bread or any other sustaining food, and we camped each night in the midst of our enemies, who were always ready to surprise us, so that we had not one hour of sleep or rest.

Were not so many miseries together enough to beat us down and crush us? Many soldiers died of hunger and exhaustion, and many others blew their brains out in despair.[26]

It may be that impatient readers will ask, 'How did you get involved in such an appalling mess?' I should have to answer them that we were not there for our own pleasure, that an army is, essentially, only an obedient and passive body and that it was not for us to question the orders of our superiors, nor the justice of the war on which we were engaged.

But these are foolish reflections. Let us continue with our journey and our story.

On the night of 28th/29th Messidor [16th/17th July 1798], exhausted by the heat, by fatigue and sleepiness, we threw ourselves to the ground, our heads pillowed on our haversacks. No sooner had we tasted the comfort of Morpheus than our ears were assaulted by cries of 'To arms! To arms!' We woke with a start and again heard the mournful sounds repeated in faltering and ghastly tones, which seemed to announce a general throat-cutting. The gurgling of the river we assumed to be the groans of our dying comrades. Shots could be heard all around us even in the camp itself. The Mameluks are among us, we cried, all is lost; let us sell our lives dearly! Obsessed with this idea, we seized our guns and were ready for battle in an instant.

This alarm had no dire consequences. A few Mameluks, prowling around the camp, had been seen by our outposts, which they had hoped to surprise asleep. Bullets whistling about their ears informed them that not all of us in camp were sleeping. In vain did these barbarians repeat their monkey-tricks in the shadows; we were finally rid of them at the cost of our sleep.

On the following day (29th Messidor) we continued our advance on Cairo, with no other rations than three biscuits per man. However, an enemy ship captured on the Nile provided us with a further supply of biscuits of the very worst quality, extremely salt, made out of bad flour and

---

[26] Two brothers, tying themselves together, jumped to their deaths in the Nile.

old fat which had been scorned by the rats. One would have to be in our situation to have the stomach to eat them. There was no occasion, however, to fear indigestion as each man received only twelve ounces as his share. As we did not know when we might receive any more we were careful not to eat them at once; we divided them into several portions, one for each day as long as they lasted. In other words we rationed ourselves. I myself divided mine into three lots of four ounces each, which would sustain me for three days. I took care, before eating, to soak each one in water for at least an hour to soften and desalt it a little. On this day we arrived at Ouârdan[27] where we remained on the 30th in a grove of palm trees.

The biscuits we had received were far from having satisfied our bodies, so long starved of proper food. However, necessity is the mother of invention and this came to our aid. The soldiers found means to grind the corn and make bread, as in Europe, and this helped us a little. Apart from this we found delicious and abundant refreshment in the watermelons, which since leaving Alexandria had often been of great help. These were a type of melon which contained a sweet and nourishing juice. I feel sure that half the Army owed their lives to these melons and to the blessed waters of the Nile.

At Ouârdan, the Commanding General came to inspect the Army; he went among our ranks and chatted familiarly with the soldiers, who did not hesitate to complain and make clear to him the depth of their misery. He was not unaware of this, but wished to ascertain the morale of the army. To cheer them up and give them courage he was lavish with his promises. A few more days, he told them, and you will have an abundance of everything in the capital of Egypt: white bread, good meat, excellent wine, sugar, coffee etc. With this we had to be content.

As soon as the army was a little refreshed by its stay in Ouârdan, the order was received to continue on its wearisome way, heading always towards Cairo. It was the first day of Thermidor, Year VI [20th July 1798]. On this, the first day, the fatigue was less than previously, a day of rest having alleviated the burden. It was not so on the second day. The heat of the sun seemed to burn twice as fiercely as we advanced and the air we breathed was scorching, so that we again lost more of our unhappy comrades.

---

[27] Moiret writes: 'It was at Ouârdan that Father Sicard burned so many ancient manuscript hidden in a dovecote, under the pretext that they were books of magic.'

CHAPTER III

On the 2nd Thermidor (21st July) we did not go far before meeting some of the outposts of Murad Bey's army. We pushed them before us, from village to village, towards the main body of their army, which we started to encounter at about two in the afternoon. The heat was suffocating and we found it almost impossible to breathe. Since the morning the divisions had been marching in square formation so that, although the Nile flowed not far from the army's route, it was impossible for anyone to break away to quench his thirst.

The circumstances were such that great care was needed; moreover, we knew that the enemy was in control along the river. Nevertheless, overcome by their terrible thirst, some soldiers disobeyed their orders and ran to the river bank. They had hardly gulped down a mouthful of water before the enemy appeared. The alarm was beaten, everyone flew back to the ranks: troubles were forgotten, and the only thoughts were of the coming test of courage.

The Mameluks, entrenched at the village of Embabeh, on the bank of the Nile opposite Cairo, were drawn up behind their formidable gun emplacements. The rays of the sun, shimmering on their accoutrements and weapons, dazzled us. There they sat on their Arab horses, each armed with a London pistol and a shining carbine, making their superb damascene scimitars flash before our eyes. This impressive sight would have been enough to frighten any but a French soldier.

It was obvious from their manoeuvres that they were preparing to attack, and we, on our side, made ready to give them a hearty welcome. Their leader, Murad Bey, at the head of an elite troop of cavalry, swept down on two of our divisions (those of Reynier and Desaix), while the rest of their army menaced us, so preventing us from going to the assistance of the two generals. But our artillery held its fire until the attackers were well within range and knocked many of them over with the first discharge. The enemy hoped for better luck by attacking our rear, but our division, in square formation, again presented a formidable front and gave him the same welcome as before. Those who had not fallen wounded by the hail of bullets, retreated hastily and dared not return to the charge. Fifteen hundred Mameluks and as many *fellahin*[28] still held out in the village of Embabeh. The divisions commanded by Kléber, Bon and Menou proceeded there and burned the village. In vain the defenders performed prodigies of valour. They saw their communications cut, one after another, and lost hope, even of retreat. An offer was made to them that they should surrender and become our prisoners. They made no response, preferring to die. Our soldiers, who had, with difficulty, been restrained by their officers while the negotiations took place, now fell furiously on the village. Instead of amusing themselves by shooting, they marched right up to the field-pieces and repeatedly stabbed the gunners with bayonets and seized their guns. Those who could fled, but found themselves cut off by our divisions on the right and were repulsed by a brisk fusillade. Some were hit and fell to the dust. Others, with no hope of deliverance, flung themselves, raging, into the Nile where they drowned.

We seized forty field guns from them, as well as a good deal of baggage, munitions, food and four hundred camels laden with gold and silver. This victory, which has been called 'The Battle of the Pyramids' cost only a little French blood and, as General Berthier[29] said, no battle has ever shown more clearly the superiority of European tactics over the undisciplined courage of the Orient.

General Desaix pursued the fleeing enemy and routed Murad Bey's rear guard near Gizeh, at the mouth of the great Nile valley. The battle lasted for two hours until nightfall. Then, masters of the field, we took up our positions preparatory to crossing the Nile. There was still a threat from a handful of the enemy who looked, from the opposite bank, as if they intended to defend Cairo. But, dismayed by our success and fearing the results of resistance, they fled after burning some merchants' ships and a few fine houses belonging to them.

Some of our troops crossed the Nile and took possession of the town

---

[28] *Fellahin*: a term used to indicate the ordinary Egyptian peasants of the time.
[29] Louis Alexandre Berthier (1753–1815), later Marshal of France, Prince of Neuchâtel, Prince of Wagram; Napoleon's invaluable Chief-of-Staff.

during the night, while the rest remained on the west bank of the river to prevent any unforeseen problems arising. Three days later the rest of the army crossed the river and entered Cairo. The rule of the Mameluks was overthrown and the whole of Lower Egypt conquered.

On arrival in the town Bonaparte addressed the following proclamation to the inhabitants.

People of Cairo,
I am pleased with the way you have behaved: you have done well not to oppose me; I have come to destroy the whole race of Mameluks, to protect the commerce and the natives of the country. Let all those who are afraid be reassured, let those who have fled return to their homes, let prayers be said today as usual, as I wish them always to be said. Fear not for your women, your houses, your property, or, above all, for your religion which I love.
Bonaparte.

In this last battle we mourned only nine or ten men killed and a hundred wounded. The enemy lost at least sixteen hundred men. Justice must be done here to the bravery of the Mameluks. If their military tactics had matched their courage they would have made us pay dearly for our victory, but their inexperience guaranteed our success. Murad Bey, their commander, distinguished himself above all by his courage and coolness, but not by his military talent. It was said that he had been wounded in the head. As for us, we should have had nothing to complain of, if the Arabs, the climate, the food and the thirst had not caused us more trouble than the Mameluks.

The famous pyramids are regarded as one of the seven wonders of the world. There are three of them, of which the largest, like the others, has four faces, each turned to one of the four points of the compass. The base is a square whose side measures about 238 yards, with an area of 56,802 square yards. The faces are equilateral triangles, thus the height is $468\frac{1}{2}$ feet. The volume of the whole structure is 2,038,335 cubic feet. On the outside it is constructed in the form of steps, diminishing as it gets higher. It is built of stones of an extraordinary size, the smallest measuring 30 feet square. This type of stone is very rare in Egypt. The top of the pyramid, which from below resembles a needle point, is in fact a platform on which forty men could easily stand. Each side of this platform is about 16 feet long; one can climb there, outside the pyramid, by means of the four angles or ridges which facilitate access by their special construction.

Once up there, the men on the ground look no bigger to you than dwarves. A fine panorama is spread before you, with views of Cairo to the east as well as the course of the Nile both above and below the town. The entrance to the pyramid is through a very well built little vault, in which there are steps to assist the descent. One goes down for about five minutes and then climbs again for about the same length of time to reach the chamber called 'The Queen's Room'. This is about 20 feet square and very well constructed, but the smell of the air does not encourage you to remain there for long. It is thought that the bodies of Egyptian queens were laid to rest there. Leaving there, one climbs for seven or eight minutes through a series of vaults, access to which is quite difficult, to reach the chamber named 'The King's Room'. This is about the same size as the previous one, but in it there is a granite coffin, 6 feet long with a width and height of 3 feet. This, it is said, was intended as the burial place of the kings of the country. Finally, there is a shaft of unknown depth in there. Someone fired a pistol into it and the sound reverberated for so long that we thought the shaft must lead into vast caves.

The ancient town of Memphis is not very far from these monuments to human vanity. The two other pyramids are the same shape as the first but their height is much less. One of them is distinguished by the granite with which it is covered. Not far from these two, the ruins of several other small, fallen pyramids can still be seen and, a little further off on an isolated rock, there is the figure of an enormous sphinx.

Four miles away at a place called 'Saqqarah' remain another seven or eight pyramids, large and interesting enough to be well worth a visit; here 'mummies', or embalmed corpses which have lain preserved for many centuries, can be seen, testifying to posterity the respect in which the ancient Egyptians held the remains of their relations and loved ones.

The part of the army which had not, so far, entered Cairo remained on the left bank of the river, camped opposite the town; they suffered a great deal for two or three days from lack of necessary supplies which it had, until then, been impossible to prepare and send to them. During that time our soldiers entertained themselves by fishing out the Mameluks who had drowned in the Nile; on them they found three or four hundred gold pieces which recompensed them for the work of dragging the corpses from the water.

At last, on the 8th Thermidor [27th July], we received the order to cross the river. During the crossing a peasant informed us of a Mameluk who, in guise of a beggar, was spying on all our movements. He was arrested and was shot on the following morning at the camp which we set up at Bulaq, about a quarter of a mile from the town. From this place we were able to visit Cairo and obtain some idea of this, the capital city of Egypt. It is no longer what it once was. It is as large as Paris, and has as many people, but what people! It is inhabited by filthy men, as black as our chimney sweeps of Savoy, lazy as the scum of Naples, in fact exactly like the citizens of Alexandria of whom we have already given a picture! The streets are narrow and winding and the air is unwholesome; there is no paving and there are no lights at night. Most of the buildings are only miserable hovels; those belonging to the rich are heavy masses of stone or brick, thatched with reed matting. When they tumble in ruins they are not restored, but are abandoned and others built elsewhere. They are scarcely lit by a few narrow windows, covered with grills and placed high in the walls. There is a platform on top which may or may not have a parapet. The Beys and Mameluks who own these places nevertheless enjoy a life of Asiatic luxury supported by the sweat of a miserable and oppressed peasantry. This luxury is manifest in the superb horses with rich trappings, in the clothing of silk covered with gold and diamonds, and in the numerous wives and slaves crowded into harems or seraglios; there are certain Beys who keep as many as two hundred such individuals. They are determined to have the finest weapons, superb carbines, beautiful London pistols and damascene scimitars, of which nearly all have silver-gilt scabbards. Many of these scimitars are worth two hundred louis.

The dwellings of the extremely rich individuals in this country cannot be compared with those of the greatest in Paris, either in taste, elegance or comfort. They have no other beds than sofas magnificently upholstered and covered with a mattress; this is the most important part of the furnishing. As for the ordinary people, their beds are soon made up, for they lay on the ground on simple mats.

Their finest dishes have nothing to please the refined European. Moreover they lack that which would most delight a French guest, I mean, of course, wine, which is forbidden by their barbarous laws. There were no inns in Egypt before our arrival, and the only refreshment to be found was coffee, drunk without sugar in the Egyptian manner; and they certainly do not stint themselves of it, drinking about twenty cups each day, and this is their chief nourishment.

Since our arrival in the country, several French people have opened inns and cafés, but you visit them at your peril, for you find that the wine is considered cheap if a bottle costs ten francs, and even then it has been adulterated or is of poor quality.

The only thing we enjoyed in Cairo was riding the donkeys. We rode them to explore the city streets or visit the neighbourhood. They were to be hired everywhere, at a reasonable price. The speed at which they trotted (as did their drivers) placed them far ahead of the ones found in Europe. One could hardly compare them, except perhaps with the ones to be hired in the Rhône Valley from Lyon to Valence. It was very strange to see the French officers, and even the soldiers, tearing along the streets of Cairo on such chargers. As for the pleasures of gallantry, we found none of the opportunities which Milan, Padua, Leghorn, Rome, Verona, Graz etc. had afforded. It was neither possible nor prudent to meet the womenfolk of the rich, who were always kept locked up and in the power of jealous tyrants. There were, however, brothels, but the hideousness, the squalor and the chattering of the courtesans were enough to sicken and revolt the boldest libertine. Thus it was not difficult to restrain oneself in spite of lusty passions and the heat of the climate.

In the citadel of Cairo could be seen Joseph's well, sunk into the rock 280 feet deep and measuring 42 feet round. One could go, by easy steps, about half way down. There, there was a wheel turned by oxen, which drew water up to fill a reservoir, from which, by means of another wheel bearing containers, it was drawn to the top of the well. Oxen also turned this second wheel, near to which stood large jars by means of which water was collected. Although it came from very deep down, the water had a bitter, salty taste which was very disagreeable. The well was not called after the patriarch Joseph, the son of Jacob, but after the vizier Joseph Karacoush who built the temple of Mohammed.

Also in the citadel could be seen the ruins of what was called the Temple of Solomon. The ruins were supported by thirty marble columns which were of such an astonishing size and height as to indicate that the temple must originally have been of an extraordinary magnificence.

Between old Cairo and Gizeh was an island called Rôdah, which was made lovely with all kinds of trees and other plants. That was where the *Miqyâs* were found, wells which were used to measure the height of the Nile flood. The degrees were marked in Arab characters on a graduated scale. The inhabitants judged the fertility or otherwise of the year by the number of degrees the Nile rose. There was a Corinthian capital over the well which was supported on four marble columns and formed a roof.

It was here, on this island, that we built a windmill for our own use.

The Beys, as soon as they learned of our arrival in Egypt, had flung the Europeans who lived in Cairo into prison with the intention of massacring all of them. The reader will probably want to know the fate of these unhappy people. To satisfy this reasonable curiosity, I can answer that they owed their safety to the superstition and credulity of these tyrants of Egypt. Ibrahim Bey, one of them, the second in rank, had a wife who was highly esteemed and thought to be inspired by the Prophet. This lady, making use of an alleged prophesy of Mohammed which foretold the French capture of Egypt in 1798, stayed the hands of the Mameluks' assassins, and had their intended victims concealed in her own apartments, where they were well treated. Our arrival in Cairo ended the distress of these prisoners and restored them to liberty. What was the reason for this woman's generosity? Was it true belief in the oracles of the Prophet or perhaps a secret inclination for the warriors of a nation whose courtesy she would have appreciated and whose gratitude she would have expected. I do not know, and leave it to the judgement of the reader. Whatever her motive might have been, it is nevertheless true that it was superstition that enabled her to overcome the cruelty of those around her. So, the fanaticism which had outraged humanity elsewhere, on this occasion, came to its aid.

We remained where we were without anything of interest occurring until 13th Thermidor [31st July 1798], when we saw a number of camels approaching, carrying both men and women. We thought at first that this must be a caravan of merchandise belonging to the Mameluks. We were wrong: it was a caravan of pilgrims returning from a visit to the tomb of Mohammed in Mecca. Custom demands that all devout Muslims should go there at least once in a lifetime, just as Christians visit Calvary or the tomb of Jesus, or the shrine of St James of Compostella. The most fanatical Muslims, on their return from Mecca, would blind themselves, saying that there was nothing further to be seen after viewing the tomb of their Prophet.

This caravan comprised nearly six thousand people, as many women as men, and the same number of camels. Most of the men possessed firearms and daggers. They were astonished to find European troops in their country, but they were reassured when they found that, far from wishing to offend them, we offered help and assistance. This behaviour on our part caused them to move off peaceably to their homes.

The caravan of merchandise on which we had previously fixed great hopes soon appeared in its turn. This one did belong to the Mameluks and they were anxious to protect it from our rapacity. A few fugitives remaining from those we had defeated earlier came to meet the caravan, intending to warn them to take another route. Our General, learning of this, deployed troops to surround them and prevent their escape.

The Bedouins, who always helped those who paid them best, or rather those who gave them the best chance of looting, asked the Commandant of the French detachment to let them join in and take part in the fight against the Mameluks in return for a share in the booty. Their offer was accepted. In some circumstances any reasonable means of ensuring success may be used. *Virtus an dolus, quis in hoste requirat.* The Bedouins, working together with our troops, attacked the Mameluks escorting the caravan with great enthusiasm; the Mameluks defended themselves stubbornly and, as they had the advantage of numbers, contested the victory for some time, but our tactics decided the day. The Mameluks fled, taking with them as much of their merchandise as they could. The rest was divided, in accordance with our agreement, between the Arabs and our troops. We finally carried off a good quantity of gold and merchandise and pursued the fleeing Mameluks to the edge of the desert, into which we were wary of going.

The Mameluks left us in peace for some time, which allowed us to observe and take part in the festival (or rejoicing) in Cairo which customarily celebrated the flooding of the Nile. This occurred that year on 29th Thermidor [16th August 1798]. The ceremony was named the 'bleeding' of the Nile. When the waters reached a certain height it was a sign that the next harvest would be abundant. The most important persons in the town took part in the ceremony: they opened, or rather ordered to be opened, a canal by means of which the water poured towards the town. Immediately, widespread joy was shown in songs, laughter and rustic games. The French, wishing to win the friendship and goodwill of the local population, encouraged the general enthusiasm and happiness by providing escorts when needed and our generals appeared there in full dress uniform.

A few days after this, the anniversary of the death of Mohammed was celebrated. On this occasion the French again played a prominent part. Troops carrying their weapons and accompanied by martial music provided a wonderful spectacle. The whole city was illuminated and the leading citizens paraded through the streets wearing the insignia of their rank or function, all attended by slaves, some carrying weapons and others bearing lighted torches. The procession was led by French and Turkish bands. The cavalcade arrived in the square where a dazzling illumination representing the tomb of Mohammed appeared to be suspended in mid-air, in accordance with the belief of the common folk that the tomb was elevated to the roof of the temple in Mecca by magnetism on the day of the Prophet's death. All believers regarded this as a great miracle.

This public holiday, in which we took part only for political reasons, had not the same attraction for us as our French feast days, but at that moment the English gave us a day to remember,[30] more serious and wretched than the death of Mohammed.

In our dismay we exaggerated everything we discussed; we were even bold enough to let our grumbles be heard, 'It was madness that planned this expedition and recklessness which undertook to carry it out.' 'No', muttered others, 'It was the ambition of the Commander-in-Chief which brought us here. He came here to elevate himself to a throne built on our sweat and our blood.' Then again, 'No, it is the treason and cunning of the government', cried those who did not wish to blame our General. 'The Directory[31] feared his presence in Paris and the love his companions in toil and glory felt for him. They want to get rid of him and us as well, and to make us pay cruelly for the laurels which we won in Italy'.

---

[30] 1st August 1798: Nelson destroyed the French fleet in Aboukir Bay, thus cutting off the Army of Egypt from France.

[31] The Government of France at that time.

It was difficult to judge which of these opinions was nearest to the truth; perhaps all were equally well founded. Yet time, which little-by-little undermines and destroys even the sturdiest objects, eventually soothed our distress and banished our black thoughts. All became resigned and carried on, aware that only unfaltering courage could save us.

Nevertheless this courage was immediately put to a new test. Ophthalmia, an illness which is so common that Egypt has justly been called 'the country of the blind', now began to ravage our ranks. This brought discontent to a new pitch in the minds of many soldiers. After some months of blindness, most sufferers recovered their sight and returned to their battalions; the others remained in hospital or, when possible, were returned to France. The air of Egypt is extremely unhealthy. Every year, between the spring equinox and the summer solstice, malignant and deadly fevers abounded. In the autumn anthrax appeared, which carried off its victims in two or three days. During the winter there was smallpox, causing terrible ravages; during the time of the Nile flood most of the inhabitants suffered from a stubborn form of dysentery, caused by the water, which during that period was very salty.

For the two and a half months before the summer solstice, the Nile was stagnant; the tidal bores at the mouths of the river and the north wind which started to blow at that time of year prevented the river from flowing, and as a result the motionless water rotted.

The catastrophe which had befallen our fleet revived the hopes and the audacity of the Mameluks' supporters. Their agents worked to stir them up and it was clear that the English were at the back of it. Soon hordes of Arabs, bringing the peaceful natives with them by means of threats and terror, appeared on all sides to attack our front line troops. But, seeing that their efforts and attempted attacks were useless, they decided to stop assaulting us boldly and, instead, to surprise and cut the throats of our outlying detachments which had been dispersed in different villages. They also waged a sort of pirate's war against us on the Nile. This war, in the final analysis, was more lethal for us than a straightforward bitter fight and carried off many brave soldiers. It was at this time that a detachment of fifteen men was slaughtered in a village, together with their commanding officer and the aide-de-camp Jullien. This was a detachment of the 1st Battalion of the regiment to which I belonged.

On 9th Fructidor [26th August 1798] we were ordered to burn the village where this happened and exact a shocking revenge. We therefore embarked on the Nile at Bulaq, and landed at Alqâm on the 11th Fructidor [28th August 1798] at half past four in the morning.

We found the village deserted. All the inhabitants, the most guilty of whom would have been executed, had been warned in time of our approach and had fled. We had, therefore, to content ourselves with destroying the whole place by fire. Nevertheless, the anger of the soldiery vented itself on an old man and an old woman in whose house blood-soaked French clothing had been found – and also on the pigeons which abound in Egypt. This was the only booty we managed to carry off from this wretched village.

We note, in passing, that small game is very common in Egypt for two reasons: first because hunting is unknown and secondly because the natives do not eat wild game, so it was cheaper than vegetables and salad.

Our mission completed we re-embarked on the Nile and returned to Bulaq. There General Lanusse received the order to proceed with his division to Menouf; we set off and arrived in that town on the same day.

Menouf is below Cairo – at the beginning of the delta, practically equidistant from the two branches of the Nile. At first we regretted leaving Bulaq. Exposed to the full glare of the sun, we were unable to find any wood with which to build ourselves shelters. However, when we got to know Menouf better we were no longer sorry to be there, especially when the troops we were relieving vacated a suitable place for our camp.

There were plenty of provisions in the town, and at a reasonable price, so we enjoyed a peaceful period there and were even starting to like it when the order to leave and return to Bulaq was received. We were hopeful that we might return when the Festival of the Republic for which we were recalled was over, but we did not know for certain. Whatever might happen, we now embarked on the Nile for what was destined to be a further three days. On the 4th September there was a downpour (surprising in Egypt where it seldom rains, and in two hundred years no such phenomenon had occurred!). The Nile was then in full flood, and this caused our helmsman to leave the ordinary course of the stream and to run aground several times in the flooded fields. We were forced to take over the helm from him, and ourselves set course for Bulaq, where we arrived – with difficulty – at nine in the evening of the 5th September, whereas our comrades had been there since nine in the morning.

Our helmsman's mistakes may have been caused by his clumsiness, but I had some reason to suspect his intentions. There had been many murders resulting from the villainy of guides, and this caused me to feel extremely suspicious. I was very angry with the man and threatened him with dreadful punishments, but he disarmed me with his excuses and repeated pleas to spare him. From then on I was always on my guard against such happenings, and events proved me right.

CHAPTER IV

THE FESTIVAL OF THE REPUBLIC – SIGNS OF DISCONTENT – VINDI-
CATION FOR THE DISSENTERS – THREAT OF TURKISH RETALIATION –
JOURNEY TO DAMIETTE – THE MIRAGE – BANDITRY AND THE ASSISTANCE
OF THE GREEKS – BONAPARTE'S REPORT ON THE BATTLES OF MIT-
GAMAR AND SEDIMAN

At daybreak on the 1st Vendémiaire, Year VII [22nd September 1798], we
formed up in battle order and marched to Cairo, to Esbékieh Square,[32]
where everything had been made ready to celebrate the founding of the
Republic.

This had been announced on the previous day and was begun on the
following morning by three artillery salvoes which were echoed by the guns
of all the divisions as well as those of the Navy. A circle with a diameter of
200 yards had been marked out, whose perimeter was adorned with a
hundred and five columns from each of which flew a tricolour flag bearing
the name of a département of France. These columns were joined together
by a double garland, emblem of the indivisibility of the Republic. At one of
the entrances to the circle stood a triumphal arch which represented the
Battle of the Pyramids. Above the other was a portico on which were
written several Arabic inscriptions, notably 'God is God, and Mohammed
is his Prophet'. In the middle was an obelisk shaped like a pyramid 70 feet
high. On one of its faces could be read the words 'Hail the French
Republic', and on the opposite side, 'To the expulsion of the Mameluks'.
There were Arabic inscriptions on the other two sides. The names of the
heroes of each division who had died to free Egypt had been carefully
inscribed among the military trophies on the obelisk.

---

[32] Moiret notes: 'This place was rather low-lying, and was flooded for two or three
months of the year. It was possible to use little boats and to bathe there. We had trees
planted all around to give shade to the walk. After the water had receded, plants were
sown and it became like a garden.'

When we were all drawn up in this circle, the band played triumphal music, the warlike marches and patriotic songs which were in vogue at that time. The troops fired several times as a battalion. During this ceremony an *Adjudant-Général* stepped forward onto a platform and read us the following proclamation:

From General Headquarters, 1st Vendémiaire, VIIth Year of the French Republic, one and indivisible
Bonaparte, Commanding General

Soldiers,
We are celebrating the first day of the seventh year of the Republic. Five years ago the independence of the French people was threatened but you recaptured Toulon, and this signalled the ruin of our enemies.

One year later you vanquished the Austrians at Dego.

The following year you scaled the Alps. Two years ago you struggled at Mantua and won the famous victory of Saint-Georges. Just a year ago you were at the source of the Drave and the Isonzo[33] on your way back from Germany.

The eyes of the world, from the English, famous in art and commerce, to the appalling and ferocious Bedouin, are fixed upon you. Soldiers, your destiny is sublime, you are worthy of all you have achieved and of the opinion everyone has of you.

You will die with honour, like the heroes whose names are inscribed on this pyramid; or you will return to your fatherland, admired by all and crowned with laurels . Throughout the five months since we left Europe we have been constantly in the minds of our fellow countrymen. On this day, forty million citizens celebrate the era of democratic government; forty million citizens think of you and say – 'It is their toil, their blood to which we owe peace, tranquillity, prosperity and the blessings of civil liberty.'
Bonaparte.

The *Adjudant-Général* ended his reading with the usual cry of 'Long Live the Republic' and attempted by his gestures to encourage the soldiers to do the same. To the great surprise of the General and his staff only a very small number of voices (perhaps none) were heard to repeat the joyous cry. The almost complete silence denoted a universal discontent. In fact, the soldiers, believing themselves to have been deprived of any way of returning to their own country, learning each day of the slaughter of many of their comrades, and suffering all manner of privations, muttered and cursed those they thought to be the cause of their exile. They went so far as to accuse, to blame the inexperience, the cowardice, even the treason of the sailors who had allowed our fleet to be destroyed at Aboukir. In truth, the devotion of

---

[33] Rivers rising in the Italian Alps.

the army had always been to the fatherland, not to this or that form of government, no matter how many efforts were made to convince them that this particular government was better for France.

These grumbles were only because they thought that all our suffering and sacrifices had contributed nothing to the glory and the well-being of their beloved fatherland; the murmurs were not loud, and they were not heard by the public any more than by the superior officers. We were the only ones to hear them, placed as we were between the highest and lowest ranks of the Army. At no time did such mutterings, vague and limited as they were, ever diminish the courage of the troops; as the future would show, the grievances would fade away when the call came to march into battle. It was not mutiny nor revolution, it was simply a need to relieve their minds which caused this outpouring of ill-humour. The unfortunate who complained may certainly be excused. But back to our story . . .

The Turkish Privy Council, the leading men of each province and the magistrates of each town had been invited to the festival; they also attended a banquet provided by the Commanding General. This was the first time that the flags of France and Turkey, the Turban and the Cap of Liberty, the Koran and the Declaration of the Rights of Man had been placed together on the same altar; the first time that the circumcised and the uncircumcised had been seated at the same feast. The only difference was that the former partook of their own sweets and drinks while the latter cracked open their Bordeaux and burgundy. If the Muslims felt any temptation to break the law of the Prophet, they showed no sign of it. But their suspicion of the god of wine did not prevent them from joining the Christians in coffee and intoxicating liqueurs. The consideration and courtesy they met with on this occasion seemed to give them pleasure and to flatter their pride. After the dinner, at about four o'clock, the arena was opened for races, both on foot and on horseback. The first race on foot was awarded to a man named Pathou – a corporal in our 75th – and the first horse-race was won by M. Sucy, the pay-master, whose horse covered thirteen-hundred and fifty yards in four minutes.

When darkness fell the arena was illuminated with lamps that had been placed among the garlands, producing a delightful effect. There were fireworks at eight o'clock, These had been most elegantly designed; I have hardly ever seen anything more beautiful. In fact everything went off perfectly.

The festival was brought to an end by further fusillades of musketry and artillery, after which the troops marched away and returned to their quarters.

On the following day the corps of which my detachment was part received the order to leave immediately and proceed to Damiette, where our garrison there had been harassed by the Bedouins for several days. They had attacked on the nights of 16th and 17th September, but instead of finding our troops sunk in sleep, several of the villains met their own doom, and the others only escaped by immediate flight. They had tried several times since to avenge themselves, but always in vain. Their plan was to get rid of us in order to extort – as had previously been their custom – large payments from the townspeople. I say that this was their custom, for, under the domination of the Mameluks, and in spite of their vigilance, the Bedouins had come each year to surround the towns. They would then command the chief citizens to produce such and such a quantity of money; disobedience would result in pillage and death. It was on such tributes that their livelihood depended.

My battalion immediately embarked for the journey to Damiette, but I and several of my comrades had to remain in Cairo on administrative duties, and so were separated from it for a while. My rage and sorrow can be imagined when I heard that two captains, one lieutenant and the quartermaster of the battalion, had been murdered by the Bedouins while on the Nile! I thought that if I had been with them I could have saved them by greater prudence or courage from this dreadful fate, or, had I perished with them, I would at least have been free of the terrors which seemed to assail us from all sides.

Indeed, on 29th September we received a circular letter from the Commandant of Cairo, which warned us to be on our guard, asserting that the Turks wished to kill every Frenchman, and that our survival depended on our courage and the resolution with which we defended ourselves.

This news, together with that from Damiette, which arrived at the same time, caused us grave concern. We imagined the whole of Egypt rising up and falling upon us to crush us beneath the weight of its huge mass. Such a prospect would have been enough to freeze the blood of any army but ours, but we, having so often confronted death, saw in the storm rising round us only new opportunities to show courage and to win fresh laurels. Anyway, the miserable existence which the Army led in such a climate made it as indifferent to death as to life.

In any event, the storm dissipated on this occasion and our fear was relieved; the dire prospects were averted by the care and endless vigilance of our leaders.

When my comrades and I had finished our work in Cairo, we wished to rejoin our corps in Damiette, but our departure was opposed because of the dangers which we might encounter on the Nile. However, after a great deal of argument we obtained permission to leave and so, on the 12th Vendémiaire, Year VII [9th October 1798], we embarked with different detachments. Thanks to our careful preparations we reached Damiette without difficulty.

Our voyage, made tedious by the vigilance essential to our safety, was not without its pleasures. Both banks of the Nile offered us new views and sights. The course of the Nile is winding and each bend revealed a different prospect. We saw the distant pyramids resembling, from so far away, two mountain peaks losing themselves in cloud, like the mountains of Savoy seen from the top of Fourvières at Lyon. This sight seemed to inspire an almost religious awe, mingled with some melancholy.

On all sides we saw dovecotes, pyramidal in shape, around which flew clouds of pigeons. On our way we sailed amongst islands where the grass was lush and buffaloes were led to pasture. A herdsman, sitting astride the neck of one of the animals, rode into the water, cracking his whip and guiding the rest of the herd. The herd followed him, bellowing as they swam towards their feeding place. These animals, living by the Nile during the hot season, plunge into the water up to their shoulders, and browse on the sweet grass growing along the banks. The buffalo cows yield an abundance of rich milk which is made into excellent butter.

The dreary monotony of the endless Egyptian plains is slightly relieved by the position of the villages, placed as they are on hillocks – either natural or man–made – as well as by occasional clumps of date palms etc., and the minarets which rise above the miserable shacks of which the villages are composed.

On our way to Damiette we again noticed a phenomenon that we had seen on our first journey to Cairo. This is what happened: in the evening and the morning, the appearance of the ground is as you would expect it to be – between yourself and the last village you can see only earth. But as soon as the air warms a little in the sun and until, at nightfall, it cools off again, the ground no longer seems the same; it appears as if surrounded for a radius of about a mile by an enormous sea. The villages outside this circle seem like islands floating in the midst of the water: beneath them one can see their mirror images, upside down, as if reflected in water. A horseman galloping over the desert seems to be crossing a flooded field, and if one knew nothing of this optical illusion, one would fear for his safety. The experts call this phenomenon a 'mirage'. I leave it to them to assign a cause and explain it.

M. Monge[34] attributed this effect to a lowering of the density of the inferior layer of the atmosphere. This lowering, at first, was caused by a rise in temperature resulting from the sun heating the sand with which it was in

---

[34] Gaspard Monge (1746–1818): a mathematician included in the Expedition (see Appendix 2 and Short Biographies).

contact. At sea, this takes place when, due to certain circumstances – the action of the wind, for instance – the lower layer of the atmosphere contains more water than the other layers. It is when this happens that the rays of light emanating from the lower part of the sky, having arrived at the surface which separates the less dense layer from the ones above it, fail to penetrate this layer. The rays are reflected back and appear to the observer as an image of the sky. Thus the observer gains the impression that he is seeing part of the sky beneath the horizon; it is this part that the observer takes for water when the phenomenon occurs on land. When the same thing occurs at sea one has the impression of seeing, in the sky, all the objects which are floating on that part of the surface of the sea which is occupied by the image of the sky.

The town of Damiette, where we landed at dawn on the 12th Vendémiaire, is not large, but it is one of the busiest and the most attractive in Egypt. It curves in a semi-circle on the east bank of the Nile, two-and-a-half miles from the sea. The houses, especially those which are near the river, are very lofty, most having lovely salons placed high on terraces. Several large mosques with towering minarets are scattered through the town. The town stands on a tongue of land, bordered on the north by the sea, on the west by the Nile, and Lake Menzaleh[35] lies to the east.

This pleasant location was, however, not secure from banditry. Each year the Mameluks came and violently exacted their dues. They had hardly departed when the Bedouins would arrive and squeeze yet another contribution from the miserable inhabitants. The presence of the French did not stop them that year. Audaciously, they came as usual to gather their taxes, attempting a coup, which failed. Although they kept us permanently on edge, our vigilance disconcerted them; finally they turned their attention to Lake Menzaleh, from which they thought to land in Damiette. We countered their attack with an armed flotilla, and a very strong guard placed where we thought they would land. These precautions thwarted their efforts and proved hazardous for them. It is true that we were powerfully assisted by the Greeks living at Damiette who were on our side and who always advised us of the manoeuvres of the Bedouins and the evil plans of their partisans in the town. They were of particular service to us on the night of 29th Fructidor [15th September 1798] when, having heard the following Arabic message proclaimed from the minarets of the mosques, 'People awake! the French are to be slain', they at once warned General Vial,[36] the commanding officer. We should not have understood the

---

[35] It was at Damiette, on 4th June 1249, that St Louis landed on his first expedition to the Holy Land. He was taken prisoner at Mansourah in 1250.
[36] Honoré Vial (1766–1813), Baron from 1810, killed at Leipzig.

meaning of this Arabic cry, and it would have been disastrous had the Greeks not alerted us. General Vial took immediate action and so made the Bedouins regret that they had come too near us on Lake Menzaleh.

These, then, were the experiences of the troops of which I was part. So that the reader may know what was happening elsewhere, I will insert the following, which is a report sent from the Commander-in-Chief to the Directory.

Report to the Directory, 26th Vendémiaire, Year VII [17th October, 1798] From the Headquarters of Bonaparte, Commander General, to the executive of the Directory

Citizen Directors,
I send you herewith the details of the various battles which have taken place at various places and times against the Mameluks, sundry Arab tribes and certain rebellious villages.

Battle of Mit-Gamar

The Arabs of Dermeh were occupying the village of Doundeh, surrounded on all sides by flood water. They felt themselves to be unassailable and were infesting the Nile with their piracy and brigandage. Generals Murat[37] and Lanusse were ordered to march there and arrived on 7th Vendémiaire [28th September]. The Arabs were scattered by a fusillade. Our troops pursued them for five miles, in waist-high water. Their flocks, camels and other belongings fell to us and more than two hundred of these wretches were killed or drowned.

These Arabs are to Egypt what the Barbets[38] are to the area of Nice – with the considerable difference that instead of living in the mountains they are always on horseback and live in the desert. They pillage the Turks, the Egyptians and Europeans alike. Their savagery is equalled by the misery of the lives they lead. Their days are spent on the burning sands, beneath the fiery sun, lacking water to quench their thirst, they are pitiless and fear no god. This is the most hideous picture of primitive man imaginable.

The Battle of Sediman

On the 16th Vendémiaire [7th October] at dawn, General Desaix's division marched and soon came up with the army of Murad Bey, which had a strength of five or six thousand cavalry, mostly Arabs, and the infantry corps which guarded the entrenchments at Sediman. General Desaix formed his division, which was made up entirely of infantry, into squares, with two small groups each of two hundred men as advance guards. The Mameluks, after a

---

[37] Joachim Murat (1767–1815), later Marshal of France, Grand Duke of Berg, King of Naples; the most flamboyant of all Napoleonic cavalry leaders, who became Napoleon's brother-in-law by marriage to Caroline Bonaparte in 1800.
[38] Barbets: name for Protestants of the Piedmont and Cévennes area.

good deal of hesitation, with terrible shouts and enormous courage, finally charged the right hand platoon, which was commanded by Captain Valette of the 21st. At the same time they attacked the excellent and brave demi-brigade, the 88th, at the rear of the division. The enemy was received everywhere with the same coolness. The chasseurs of the 21st held their fire until they were within ten paces, and then used their bayonets. The heroes of this intrepid cavalry came on to die in our ranks having flung axes, clubs, rifles and pistols at the heads of our troops. Some of them, their horses having been killed, slid forward on their bellies to avoid our bayonets and slashed at the legs of our men. All to no avail; they were compelled to flee.

Our troops advanced on Sediman, in spite of four cannon whose fire was all the more dangerous because of the depth of our order of battle. However the speed of our charge was like lightening and we captured the entrench-ments, the cannon and the equipment.

Three beys of Murad Bey's army were killed and two wounded, four hundred of his elite troops died on the field of battle. Our losses were thirty men killed and ninety wounded.
Bonaparte.

CHAPTER V

NEWS OF REVOLT IN CAIRO – THE ENGLISH AS 'PRIME MOVERS' OF
UNREST – FALSE DECREES – ILLUSIONS OF EGYPT – IMMINENT CON-
VERSION OF FRENCH TROOPS – DEPARTURE FOR SYRIA – CAPITULATION OF
EL ARICH – MOIRET IS WOUNDED – NEWS OF JAFFA – JOURNEY TO GAZA

For some time, at Damiette, we enjoyed such happy tranquillity that we
began to think that our enemy's menacing plans had collapsed; we imagined
that fear of our weaponry and the fury with which we had often crushed
trouble-makers had cowed them for ever. We were wrong, for we soon
heard of a rebellion in Cairo. An interruption in communications left us in
no doubt of the accuracy of this information. It was not long before we
learned that, on 30th Vendémiaire [21st October 1798], the citizens of Cairo
had gathered in their mosques in a state of tumult and then rushed to the
houses in which the French were living; that General Dupuy[39] – the
governor of the city – having gone to confer with the commandant of the
Turkish troops to plan with him the suppression of the revolt – had been
murdered, together with his escort. We heard also that, in spite of very
frequent patrols, French people were slain whenever they were found
without protection; that the house of General Caffarelli, where the army's
engineering tools and supplies were kept, had been pillaged. Bulaq had also
been involved in the uprising, and the army bakers there had been slain, as
well as *Chef de Brigade* Sulkowski and eighteen guides[40] who were with
him. Warning cannon had been fired in vain, so that it had at last been
necessary to fire upon and bombard various parts of the town, especially the
citadel. We were told that our batteries had been chiefly concentrated on
the mosque to which the insurgents had been driven by our patrols and that

---

[39] Dominique Martin Dupuy (1767–1798), killed in the Cairo revolt.
[40] The rank *Chef de Brigade* equated to that of the colonel of an infantry regiment
during the period 1793–1803. The mounted guides were an elite cavalry escort for
Napoleon.

71

the Bedouins, having attempted to enter the city at several places to assist the uprising, had been severely punished for their temerity. Finally the revolt was suppressed and order restored by ten in the evening of 1st Brumaire [22nd October 1798].

The precautions that were taken to crush the seeds of revolt, the severity which was shown to this end, and the misery which the city had brought upon itself, so terrified those who might have been tempted, or frenzied enough, to attempt further insurrection, that they did not again forget their duty. Fortunately for us! For we knew that all were ready to rebel if the attempt at Cairo had succeeded. The loss of life amongst the Turks was considerable, mainly at Bulaq, which was devastated by our fleet on the Nile close to this suburb.

Hardly had this tempest abated when another blew up in Lower Egypt. The English, who had received reinforcements under Russian and Turkish flags, attempted a landing at Aboukir. It did not succeed. This latest attempt showed us clearly who were the authors and prime movers of the general unrest which threatened us on all sides. Agents of the English, together with those of the Mameluks, overran Egypt, handing out gold, making promises and sowing terror. It was thus, with corruption, that they contrived skilfully to rouse the Arabs and the Egyptians against us. They published false decrees everywhere, claiming them to have come from the Sublime Porte,[41] in which it was stated that we had come to Egypt against the wishes of the Almighty, and that the Porte had sent a fleet against us which, together with the English squadron, had already recaptured Alexandria.

Santhoubard played a very active role in these manoeuvres. This Santhourbard had for a long while claimed the position of Governor of Damiette and its surrounding area. The Mameluks, having been unable to stop him, left him alone to enjoy his usurpation, demanding a tribute of five hundred thousand francs, which he paid them. This adventurer had equipped a little fleet on the lake which was composed of a mob of Egyptians who had been led astray by the decrees and who came to harass Damiette from time to time.

The style in which these decrees were written and the way in which the French Army was depicted, compel me to include one here:

Decree of the Grand Vizir
To The Inhabitants of El Arich and To The People of Egypt

We have to warn you that the Sublime Porte has been informed of the intrusion into Egypt of French mischief-making which claims authority by

---

[41] Head of the Ottoman Empire, Sultan Selim III.

means of false decrees (not issued by the Sublime Porte), as well as by counterfeit letters in the name of distinguished personages, to make it appear that they have been authorised to expel the princes of Egypt and deliver you from their oppression.

Their plans are cloaked in lies and villainy. They have captured Alexandria, they have imposed their rule over the whole province of Egypt, where they have spread their poison among the inhabitants of the country. Now they are unmasked. Their evil intentions are revealed in the letters which they have sent back to their own country, and which have, mercifully, been intercepted and translated by the sovereign power, which has been careful to warn the Arabs, and to inform them of the enemy's plans. These plans are not only to take over Egypt, but also to conquer Syria and Persia. (May God preserve us from such a miserable fate!)

Today they flatter and seduce you with their gifts; but as soon as they know themselves to be safely established then they will force you to return their gifts a hundred-fold, then they will seize the goods of true believers and enslave their wives and children, then will your blood be spilled. (May the Almighty preserve us!) But, in order to be saved, our law must be the word of God, which decrees that wealth be sacrificed in his service.

Mindful of this commandment, the Sublime Porte, appointed by the power of the King of kings, sovereign of heroes and victors, king of the two seas and the two lands, our master of the world, whose glory God increases through the intercession of his Prophet and Elijah, placing his trust in God and secure in that confidence which comes only to those who rely on God, has declared war on his enemies. Entrusted with this task by our King, the ruler of our fortune, and by the great lords of the court, we have recruited vast numbers of troops from amongst the Turks, the Greeks and the Persians.

Supplied with all our needs, with, we trust, enough weapons and ammunition to crush the enemy, we shall leave the court of the Sublime Porte, with these warriors, numberless as the grains of sand on the seashore, hoping, with the help of God, to destroy for all time these infidel usurpers and deliver the true believers from their domination. Other Christian powers have declared war and hatred upon these usurpers, for they have profaned churches, burned books, massacred priests, their holy men and their king, they have pronounced themselves to be the enemy of all the Christian kingdoms which they have savaged like dogs. At this moment English and Russian ships are ready to assist the Navy of the Porte: help will be given on land; these two powers are now joined in friendship on the basis of their new treaty of alliance with the Sublime Porte.

We are now, by the grace of God, at Damascus, with our victorious troops, and advance towards you with a powerful train of artillery and everything needed for victory. People of Mohammed, turn your faces from these infidels, unite with God and his Prophet, mindful of the example of your fathers and mothers. Send to the Arabs and to the people of the country, call upon them to unite and may a holy uprising reinforce your zeal, our efforts, and the aspiration of your King (this is the most sacred of the duties of our religion). Do not listen to the cunning proclamations of infidels, for they are filled with lies and traps and there is no hope for such people. When we reach them, they will become, with God's help, the miserable victims of our gallant warriors.

As soon as you have read and understood this order, join with your neighbours to resist the infidels, be careful not to disobey, lest you should be punished in this world and the next.

Greetings,

(The signatures follow.)

Although this sort of proclamation was designed to provoke the most venomous reaction against us, to excite religious fanaticism amongst the different inhabitants of Egypt, who had no other bond than the law of Mohammed, to make us execrated as the enemies of all religion, even of our own, and depict us as engaged in perpetual war against all the kingdoms of Christendom, yet it did not produce the effect intended by those who had composed and published it. However, it did make clear to us the extent of the dangers which surrounded us, and the impossibility either of returning to our own country or of holding on to our conquests here if reinforcements were not sent from France. For, even if we could resist our enemies, how could we guard ourselves against the plague, that terrible scourge which ravages Egypt each year? Would that not thin our ranks even more effectively than the armies of the Muslims? If France herself should be attacked, and the peace which reigned when we left should be violated, how could we return to give the help vital to her own defence? Such were the thoughts which occupied our minds at this distressing time. But soon courage gained the upper hand and we told ourselves that our salvation must lie in hoping for nothing, but leaving our destiny in the hands of fate. Then we comforted ourselves with the thought that we might perhaps establish a colony in Egypt, and on this foundation we built the most delightful fantasies. By seizing the Suez isthmus and establishing fortifications there at suitable places, we would erect an insurmountable barrier against the Pasha of Syria and the Grand Vizier, who were threatening to attack us, and by the restoration of the Suez Canal we would provide free communication between the Mediterranean and the Red Sea. Egypt would become the warehouse of Europe and Asia. Our ships would no longer be obliged to pass through the dangerous Straits of Gibraltar nor to make the immense voyage round the Cape of Good Hope. We would recruit to our army the young men of the country, and instruct them in the use of weapons; their families would learn to favour us, as we brought them ease and tranquillity and respected their traditions. The population would grow in happiness and wealth. Each one of us would take over a farm, a Mameluk estate, which we should then cultivate in the French manner. We would clean the irrigation canals as well as Lake Moeris. We would improve the topsoil with numerous plantations of perennial trees, whose foliage would shelter us from the heat of the sun, and Egypt would, once again, become the granary of Europe as it had been at the time of the Roman Empire. We would rebuild the ruined monuments of old; our scholars would decipher the writings with which they are covered and thus unravel the mysteries of ancient history. And so Egypt would again become the homeland of art and of science.

The soil of this country is naturally rich and fertile. Everything that is desired can be grown: rice, corn, coffee, sugar, tobacco, indigo etc. Under our care these commodities would thrive, and we could surpass the output of our colonies which had been taken from us. If vines and garden vegetables are not common here it is because their cultivation is neglected. In the time of the Pharaohs there was no lack of them and the Israelites in the desert of Sinai longed for the onions of Egypt.

We were all the more inclined to entertain these wonderful illusions as all that our leaders did seemed to point in that direction. Indeed, our General, having arrived at Suez with the troops and the scholars attached to the expedition, took over the town of that name. They had found and drawn up a map of the traces of the old canal. The General had established easy transport from Suez to Cairo, and to Belbeiss; the arrangements he had made were such as would, in a short time, return its ancient splendour to Suez. During his stay he had made an alliance with the Arabs of Tor, at their request, and had welcomed them as friends of the Republic. For the rest, the organisations he had set up at various places, the system of government, and the work which had been put in hand to fortify and maintain us in the country, all tended to persuade us that we were to become colonists on the banks of the Nile.

While we thus bore our hopes and opinions towards an uncertain future, a rumour began, which was quickly confirmed, that we were to leave for Syria where the Pasha (Djezzar – who was called 'the Butcher') was gathering a large force against us. In this we saw only the prospect of new glory, and at the same time limitless toil. Nothing was neglected in the preparations for such an expedition, and work went briskly forward during the months of Frimaire and Nivôse.[42] This season did not prevent the outbreak of a malignant fever, which struck chiefly in Alexandria and Damiette and robbed us of many comrades. This horrible disease carried off its victims within four or five days. Nevertheless, with skill, the ravages

---

[42] 21st November to 19th January – the months of frost and snow, as reflected by the French Revolutionary Calendar (officially inaugurated in 1793).

of the illness were halted and finally cleared up. At this time, that is to say, after the suppression of the Cairo revolt, Bonaparte published the following proclamation:

To the Inhabitants of Cairo

Wicked men have led some of you astray; they have perished. God has commanded me to be kind and merciful to the people; I have been kind and merciful to you. I was angry with you because of the revolt. I have deprived you for two months of your Divan,[43] but today it is restored. Your good behaviour has wiped out the stain of your revolt.

Cherifs,[44] Ulémas,[45] and those who speak in the mosques be well aware that any who become my enemies through foolishness shall find no refuge in this world or the next. Can there exist a man so blind that he cannot see that destiny itself directs my actions? Can there be anyone so incredulous as to doubt that everything in the vast universe is subject to the rule of destiny?

Let the people know that, since the creation of the world, it is written that, having destroyed the enemies of Islam and torn down the crosses, I shall come from the distant West to fulfil the task allotted to me. Let the people understand, as it is written in more than twenty places in the holy book of the Koran, that that which is happening has been foreseen, and that which is to come has also been made clear. Those who now are only restrained by fear of our power from cursing us will change. For in imploring heaven to destroy us, they are calling down their own damnation. Let true believers pray that our arms may prosper.

I am able to demand from each one of you an explanation for even the most secret wishes of your heart; for I know everything, even those things which you have not told anyone. But a day will come when the world will see clearly that my actions are governed by a superior power and that no human effort can prevail against me. Happy are those who are the first to espouse my cause in good faith.

Bonaparte.

The soothsayers of Cairo, perhaps because they were first deceived by these extraordinary words, or perhaps because they had been secretly won over by certain little gifts, agreed entirely with our General, and helped considerably to calm the unrest which had been reduced but not dispelled among the population. They mysteriously predicted that the French 'Sultan' was about to be circumcised, would adopt the turban and the religion of Mohammed, and his entire army would follow his example; and advised that the homage due to such a great conqueror and to the heroes

---

[43] The governing council. Napoleon had arrested the Turkish governor and the high priest during the revolt.
[44] Arabian princes, descendants of Mohammed.
[45] Mohammedan doctor of law or theology.

around him required obedience, or at least respect. Most of our soldiers would not have despised the paradise of the Prophet, on condition that they were promised the opportunity of cultivating burgundy and champagne there, and as long as they were exempt from the ceremony of initiation. But as they were quite sure that they would not be allowed all these dispensations, they contented themselves with discussing the style and the aim of this proclamation. Many laughed at it. The philosophers, those we called the freethinkers, jeered, or, shrugging their shoulders, announced that they had not shaken off the prejudices of Europe only to adopt those of the Orient, and that only the truth should be spoken to the people. Those of a political bent argued that, on the contrary, the safety of the army demanded that such things should be done; that the Romans in extending their conquests beyond their own frontiers made no effort to change the morals, customs, laws or religions of the conquered peoples, that, far from imposing on them the gods of the Capitol, had, on the contrary, established therein the gods of Athens and Carthage. All the army came round to this last opinion which certainly was that of the Commander-in-Chief. As for the prophetic part of this proclamation, time alone would show, and what followed supplied us with part of the answer to the riddle.

Before our departure for Syria, a regiment mounted on dromedaries was formed and this proved to be of great use. Dromedaries are a kind of camel and are very strong and tireless. They are able to travel twenty miles a day with neither food nor water, and can carry two men as well as provisions and other items. Their riders were clad in Arab gowns and turbans. This innovation confirmed, in the minds of the Muslims, the prediction of their soothsayers, and almost made us believe in our imminent conversion. Meanwhile, my battalion received orders to set out for Syria. It left Damiette on the 2nd Pluviôse, of the Year VII [21st January 1799], embarked on Lake Menzaleh, and on the 4th dropped anchor at Mont-Farrégé to await the rest of the convoy at the old mouth of the Nile, which is named Tanitique. When the convoy arrived, we again set sail and in the evening reached a village on the coast called Tineh; from here we set off into the desert. As is always the case in a desert there was no trace of a path. My servant lost sight of the column and wandered off into this world of sand. When night fell with no sign of my servant I was convinced that he had been robbed by Arabs, that the donkey and my belongings which had been entrusted to him had been seized by them and he himself slaughtered. I continued on my way, resigning myself to this new sacrifice, and arrived at eleven o'clock with my corps at Katieh,[46] which was the assembly point for troops forming the advance guard of the Army of Syria.

---

[46] This consisted of cisterns surrounded by palm trees.

Imagine my surprise when on the following morning I saw my servant arrive, safe and sound, with all my belongings! How had he escaped the rapacious and ferocious Bedouins who infest the desert and render it impassable? He explained it to me thus: 'After leaving you', he said, 'I stumbled upon an the tent of an Arab chieftain and sat down to rest in this shelter. Soon afterwards the owner arrived and I begged, in Arabic, for hospitality. He replied "You are lucky to have found my tent, it is your guarantee of safety for the laws of hospitality are sacred to us". Refreshment was offered to me and to my beast and we were sent on our way with good wishes for our safety. "Go that way", the sheikh told me, "do not wander off, either to the right or to the left, for if I, or any of my people, should meet you away from that path, nothing could prevent our harming you". As you will imagine, sir, I followed the path he pointed out very carefully indeed. In fact I met no one, and here I am, as you see.'

He was luckier than a detachment of my battalion, commanded by a captain and a second lieutenant, which had been escorting a convoy of supplies. They were attacked in the desert on the 10th, two miles from Katieh, by a horde of brigands who, being superior in numbers, wounded the captain, killed three men and wounded forty others as well as making off with the convoy.

On 16th Pluviôse [4th February 1799], at eleven in the evening, we went back from Katieh to Tineh to look for a convoy of supplies and artillery. The darkness of the night caused us to lose our way in the desert and, having marched continuously, we found ourselves at dawn one and a half miles from our departure point. Despite our extreme weariness, we continued on our way and arrived back at Katieh in the evening, where new orders to leave awaited us. We left once more in the morning and camped six miles away. We found some brackish water there with which we quenched our desperate thirst.

On the 19th Pluviôse we marched eight miles across the burning sand without finding so much as a drop of water, either on our way or at our resting place. There, the soldiers, who until then had shown restraint, threw themselves onto the goatskins (of water) and prevented us from giving out equal shares.

On the 20th we were tormented both by thirst and by the Mameluks. Our pursuit of them enfeebled us; half of the column collapsed with exhaustion, and several soldiers remained lying without movement or life. In the evening we reached a cistern and, as there was not enough water for everyone, we dug up the earth around, which seemed to be damp, and sufficient water was obtained to quench our thirst. This water, vile as it was, yet seemed more delicious than the finest wine in the world. As soon as we had satisfied our thirst we again became our usual cheerful selves and forgot our past miseries. Little jokes, teasing words and bawdy suggestions helped us along and brought us to a grove of palm trees near El Arich, about a mile from the sea. We took up positions, intending to capture the place. The attack was postponed until the morrow. I do not know by what folly it had been assumed that this place was nothing but a cluster of old hovels weakly defended by few of the enemy. This error cost us rather dearly, for General Reynier, commanding the advance guard, having fired about thirty cannon shots at these supposed hovels without reply from the enemy, fell into the trap. Indeed, the speed of the charge brought us quickly to our goal when our eyes were opened and we saw, rather too late, that we were confronting a formidable fort surrounded by a very high wall which had been concealed by a village or huddle of hovels filled with armed men. They allowed us to come up to them and they assailed us with a hailstorm of bullets; they fired on us from all sides, so that we could not even see where the shots were coming from. We fought back stubbornly but were forced to give way to their superior numbers and strong position. This lack of foresight and neglect of sensible precautions put three hundred men out of action – a hundred killed and two hundred wounded. I was among the latter: a ball broke a bone in my right foot. The enemy also lost many men. This unfortunate encounter, which made an assault on the fort too dangerous, reduced us to the necessity of blockading it until further troops arrived. Our situation was thus far from agreeable. On one hand we were short of supplies and on the other hand we were constantly plagued by six hundred mounted Mameluks and three hundred on foot, who were attempting to introduce provisions into the fort. Continually under arms, we hardly knew what positions to take up. Only the field hospital, though exposed to many dangers, remained immobile, for the nature of their wounds made it impossible to move most of the injured. Throughout the siege they were in danger of slaughter a thousand times – moments of terror when one dies a hundred times, seeing no end to one's agony! Meanwhile hunger made itself felt more and more. We were forced to eat the camels, the horses, anything we could find while, beneath our very eyes, the Mameluks kept control of a superb convoy of supplies. For us this was the torment of Tantalus; the camp had to be captured.

So this is what was done on 27th Pluviôse [15th February 1799], at dawn. The enemy were surprised in their camp with such suddenness and vigour that they had barely enough time to mount their horses and flee, leaving behind all their food and baggage for us. Many of their horses having escaped their control, their cavalrymen fell into ours. Our pursuit of the rest of them resulted in the capture of a dozen of their flags and the death of one of their most important Beys. They were so thunderstruck by this experience that they stopped prowling around and swooping down on us as they had been doing. This capture relieved us and we were even ready to wait for a few more days. As the besieged refused to surrender the fort and capitulate, we considered how to subdue them. Mines were laid to blow them up, but their counter-mines foiled our schemes.

At last, finding themselves abandoned by the Mameluks, they entered into negotiations on the arrival of the Commanding General, who had brought us strong reinforcements; but, not wishing to accept our conditions, they announced that they would withstand our attack.

We gave the fort a terrible pounding with shells and bombs, until they decided to agree to our proposals. They surrendered on 2nd Ventôse [20th February 1799] at eleven in the evening, and handed over this wretched citadel which they had defended with a handful of men of different races, who numbered at most a hundred and fifty. The Commanding General hoped to obtain some advantage for us from this; having persuaded their leaders to join us, he took them into his service and pay, formed them into companies and gave each particular duties.

The operation on my foot to remove the bullet and the resulting pain made it impossible for me to leave when my brigade moved off on 3rd Ventôse, as part of General Kléber's advance guard. Thus, I was compelled to remain in the field hospital established at El Arich, in a barren countryside, empty of everything, sixty miles from Cairo and fifty from Gaza. Our only supplies had to come from Katieh, and this resource soon dried up as provisions in Katieh were depleted day by day. So here we were, once more a prey to hunger, once more condemned to eat camel flesh which was again in continual requisition. It would certainly have been the turn of my own animal if the arrival of a convoy had not saved it.

At last, on 11th Ventôse [1st March], we received some welcome news. Gaza had surrendered. After that we were a little better cared for; we received a pound of biscuit and a morsel of camel meat as our daily ration. Mean and coarse as it was, we were happy, for it is true that even the slightest improvement is pleasant when one has been subjected to real hardship.

Despite our sufferings and the dreadful boredom which consumed us, we still enjoyed a measure of peace, but, at midnight on 10th Ventôse, we were woken by a general alarm. An alert at this hour! An omen of new problems, an unexpected attack ... Yes, the Bedouins had forced their way into tents occupied by the sick near the fortress walls and had seized all the arms they could find. The opposition they met had prevented them from doing more, but after this the remainder of the sick were carried into the fort itself, where they could be protected from the barbarous attacks of these raiders. We had thought that these plundering bandits operated only in Egypt; we were mistaken. Several events proved to us that Syria shared this dangerous honour. Every convoy was attacked on its way to us. Even the baggage train of the Commander-in-Chief and the army treasury were attacked a few miles from Gaza, but without success.

The news of the taking of Jaffa reached us at El Arich on 24th Ventôse [14th March 1799]. This is a little town in Syria which had been fortified and defended by seven thousand men. As they had forced us to attack it and had murdered the person sent to parley with them, they were all shot with the exception of two hundred Egyptians who were taken to Cairo. This town was taken by General Kléber's division.

The forts were then occupied by our troops, who found there forty cannon which the Sultan had sent to Djezzar Pasha. After this General Kléber proceeded to Haïfa and captured it. He had no need to come to blows: the enemy abandoned the place at his approach. The army found a huge supply of provisions there.

The goal of the expedition into Syria was the capture of St Jean-d'Acre,[47] a vital position for the domination of Egypt. The victories we had won so far were wonderful omens, but no guarantee of ultimate success. St Jean-d'Acre, residence of the Pasha, was bigger, better fortified and consequently better guarded than any of the towns which we had previously overcome. It was a safe gamble that this place would put up a long resistance and that we should lose many men there. The future would tell whether our fears and apprehensions were well founded or not.

As for me, weak from my diet of biscuits, camel meat and a little rice, and longing to take part in the dangers and glories of my comrades in arms, I made up my mind to leave the desert of El Arich. My eyes, which had grown weary looking at nothing but heaps of burning sand, were soon refreshed by the sight of fields rich in Ceres' bounty, green hillsides sprinkled with poppies and a thousand perfumed flowers. My companions on this journey shared my feelings and my great happiness. As we journeyed we learned that this cultivated countryside, with its rich pasture and flowery hillsides, belonged to the nomadic Arabs who wandered here and there with no other shelter than holes scratched in the sand.

It was on the 1st Germinal [21st March] that these welcome sights, unexpected as they were, first presented themselves to my eyes, which were wearied of the monotony of the desert. We were hoping to find the water we had lacked on the journey, when, in the evening, we should reach a cistern of which we had heard, but we missed it, and wandered for some time vainly looking for it. At last we found it and experienced the great pleasure of quenching our thirst and watering our mounts. We camped and slept in a barley field where our horses and camels grazed and enjoyed a good feed.

---

[47] St Jean-d'Acre: Ptolemais of antiquity, or Akko during the Crusades.

There, all through the night, we heard the Bedouins mimicking the cry of a fox, which was their agreed way of communicating, either to gather together or to give warning of an attack. Our numbers discouraged them, no doubt, for they made no attempt on us and we slept in peace.

CHAPTER VI

SUDDEN FEVER – ORDER TO EVACUATE SYRIA – AGONISING JOURNEY
ACROSS THE DESERT – POOR ADMINISTRATION AT SEA – MARCH
AGAINST THE ANGEL EL-MAHDY – FRENCH OCCUPATION OF KOSSEIR
'ASSURES' POSSESSION OF EGYPT – BONAPARTE ENTERS CAIRO –
DESAIX'S WAR AGAINST MURAD BEY

On 2nd Germinal [22nd March 1799], after marching for an hour, we
arrived at the two columns which separate Africa from Asia. These seemed
to us to be placed obliquely – one facing towards the Red Sea and the other
towards the Mediterranean. A little further on we came across the Rapha
wells. In spite of being amazingly deep, the water in them tasted unpleasant,
but being thirsty we drank it nevertheless.

Three miles beyond the wells we found a fort and a village, surrounded
by fruit trees, the very sight of which gave us pleasure; the further we went
the more cultivated land we found. Finally, we reached Gaza which, surrounded as it was by fine olive trees, was a delightful sight. My wound
prevented me from going further and I went into hospital the same day –
2nd Germinal of the Year VII.

My longing to leave the abominable fort at El Arich had made me believe
myself cured, but how wrong I was! One day, I decided to leave the hospital
at Gaza, but after only a few paces outside tiredness and pain made me
realise that another piece of lead still remained in the sole of my foot. To get
it out a further incision had to be made, which, nevertheless, healed after
only a few days. Bored with being shut up for so long, I made one more
attempt to go for a walk, but putting my weight on the foot revealed yet
another splinter which had to be removed. This was only the start of a more
serious illness which threatened my very life. On the same day as this
second outing I was attacked by a violent fever. A bubo in my armpit alerted
me to the danger I was in and the type of illness from which I suffered. The
following morning – 19th Germinal [8th April 1799] – I asked to see the
Surgeon-Major, but was told that he was sick of the same malady that

afflicted me. I asked for a doctor, but the answer was 'He has anthrax'. Then I asked for the director of the hospital and a surgeon, only to receive the same response. I was in dire need of medicine, so I sent for an apothecary and he dragged himself to me, as well as he was able, to tell me that he too was infected with the same disease.

He advised me to make myself vomit and sweat and added that he was about to do the same thing. I followed his council and was the better for it. When my delirium and exhaustion passed, I demanded news of my six comrades who had been with me on the journey. All were dead with the exception of the apothecary who, nevertheless, followed them to the grave four days later. After this, the disease raged with redoubled violence. I saw many comrades perish around me, men whose memories will forever be dear to me, and whose loss I still regret. My servant, a fine young man, whose care of me had perhaps saved my life, was unable to save his own: he succumbed, before my eyes, after only three days. Of the three hundred French stationed in this town, two-thirds at least perished with six weeks, victims of this scourge.

Fear of contagion caused the hospital to be placed in quarantine. I soon left, but was then isolated and under observation for fifteen days. I remained unwillingly at Gaza while awaiting my return to health. I say unwillingly, for our position there was always dangerous.

All that time our thoughts and hopes were with the army surrounding Acre: we longed for news of them. The following adventure gave me a way of discovering their difficult circumstances.

On the 4th Prairial [23rd May 1799], the Commandant of the province, together with his staff officer, rode to the old port at Gaza to inspect a Greek boat laden with provisions for us. He invited me to go with him which I gladly did. When we reached the seashore we observed six sails in the distance, which cheered us up. If they were French, we told ourselves, this would mean that Acre had fallen. If they were English it would show that they had been driven out of that town, and were retreating. Deceived by this hopeful fallacy, we awaited their arrival impatiently. They did not keep us long in suspense. A frigate, having approached to within cannon shot, saluted us with a most uncivil broadside and a brig bestowed the same courtesy on the Greek ship, forcing it to strike its flag. Lacking any means of defending ourselves, and in an extremely exposed position, we pulled ourselves together and departed for Gaza, bitterly disappointed at having witnessed the loss of the provisions intended for us. As we went along we came to the conclusion that French forces must have taken Acre and driven the English out, as the latter had appeared in an area where they were not expected to be. Vain hope! Disastrous illusion! On reaching Gaza the first person I saw was a wounded soldier, coming, I thought, from the army.

'So', I shouted 'Acre is taken?' 'No', he replied, 'We are evacuating Syria'. This answer acted on me like the sight of the Medusa's head. I hadn't the heart to ask him any more. A few hours later I learned the full extent of our misfortune. A convoy of wounded started to arrive, and this was succeeded by many more, arriving continually. I heard that, after a thousand acts of valour by our brave soldiers, and after many attacks costing the lives of many good soldiers and gallant officers of high rank, we had been forced to abandon the siege. I learned that a flotilla bringing us supplies and siege guns had been intercepted at sea by the English. These supplies, which had been intended for the destruction of Acre,[48] were then used against us in its defence. This loss of ours gave the enemy more help than the redoubts and fortifications of the city, for it was impossible for us to achieve real success against a fortified town without the use of powerful artillery. In any case, the army was not sufficiently large to be able to afford the sacrifice of the number of men required to storm the place.

A young French emigré (who had been a fellow student with Napoleon at Military College) had flung himself into the battle to direct operations, using the new tactics. The extraordinary prospect of these old school-fellows fighting each other, for utterly different causes, was too remarkable to escape the attention of the French troops. They were absorbed by it, and wished only that the young man – Colonel Phélippeaux – could have used his talents in the service of our country against the English, to whom he had pledged allegiance. He might then have rivalled the glory of his antagonist, or even surpassed it as he did at St Jean-d'Acre where, they say, he lies buried. News of our retreat and return to Egypt was officially announced to us in the following notice:

General Headquarters at Acre, 28th Floréal, Year VII [17th May 1799]
Bonaparte, Commanding General

Soldiers,
You have crossed the desert separating Africa from Asia more speedily than an Arab army. The army which was on its way to invade Egypt is destroyed. You have captured its General, its equipment, baggage, water containers and camels. You have gained possession of all the forts guarding the desert wells.

You have routed, on the field of Mount Tabor, that horde gathered from all over Asia in the hope of plundering Egypt.

The thirty ships you saw arriving at Acre two days ago were carrying the army intended to besiege Alexandria but, forced to hurry back to Acre, their plans ended there. Some of their flags will embellish your entry into Egypt. Finally, having, with only a handful of men, kept the war alive in the heart of

---

[48] Here Moiret reflects upon Acre's former relevance to French and British designs: she was captured during the Third Crusade by Philippe Auguste and Richard Coeur de Lion.

Syria, taken forty field-pieces, fifty flags, captured six thousand prisoners and razed the fortifications of Gaza, Jaffa, Haïfa, we shall return to Egypt. We are recalled there because it is the time of year when landings may take place.

A few days more, and you would have had the hope of seizing the Pasha himself in his own palace. But, at this particular season, the taking of a fortress in Acre is not worth the loss of those days. Also, the brave men who I might have lost there are today needed for more vital operations. Soldiers, ours is a profession which must endure weariness and danger. Having ensured that the East is no longer able to take action against our campaign, we must, perhaps, now repel the attempts of some in the West. You will find there yet another opportunity to win glory, and if, in all these battles, each day is marked by the death of a hero, then new men of valour must step forward, in their turn, to take their place in the ranks of those few who give inspiration in danger and ensure victory.

Bonaparte and General of Division, Chief of Staff, Alexandre Berthier.

When we read this, we exclaimed: 'There is now no doubt that we must return across that terrible desert where we suffered so much'. It being later in the season the heat would be even worse, water scarcer, and, after four months of unspeakable toil and privations of every sort, the strength of the men less. We would have more wounded to carry with us, to say nothing of those stricken with the plague. Dear God, what a dreadful journey! Also, could we be sure that we should not be harassed on our march? It was difficult to think so. Never mind. The order had been given and must be obeyed.

So the wounded continued to move forward, convoy after convoy in detachments. After them came the army, marching in divisions. As I was not yet perfectly recovered, I did not want to wait for my division, which was in the rear guard. I left Gaza, therefore, before them on the 12th Prairial [31st May 1799]. This was not a long day and it was easy to endure the fatigue. On the 13th thirst began to be troublesome but we quenched it in the evening, when we arrived at El Arich. We left again at midday on 14th and were able to find water. This was the more astonishing as we had found none in the same place on our first journey. I feel I must point out here that thirst made us forget the hunger which would otherwise hardly have been satisfied with a few pieces of biscuit. We had more trouble on the 15th. The wounded, the plague-stricken and, indeed, many other soldiers, unable to endure the torments of thirst, died here in this dreadful desert. The drought had almost dried up the well which we expected to find there. On the 16th there was the same suffering and the same loss of life. On that day we reached Katieh, where there was an abundance of water. I decided to await my brigade, which arrived on the 17th.

While it was wonderful to greet and embrace many of my good friends, yet it was wretched indeed to find how many of them had succumbed, either to the fatigues of the march or in battle. Those who did rush to greet me were so exhausted, their appearance so altered that, after the three months separation, I hardly recognised those who had once been well-known to me. It was from them, as we talked together, that I learned in detail exactly how the army had suffered in Syria: the death of officers I had known, the numerous attacks made on St Jean-d'Acre, always without much success, the way in which our demi-brigade, ever worthy of the name 'Invincible' – which it had received in Italy – had behaved during the expedition and the number of brave soldiers lost to it, and finally the details of the evacuation. They did not leave me in ignorance of the fate of the plague-stricken they were forced to abandon by the wayside to the fury of a savage and barbarous enemy, or of our cannons which they left behind, lacking the means to transport them. What cruel fate! What wretched thoughts! O, Humanity, are Frenchmen doomed, here, far across the sea, to degrade your sacred name? Deadly ambition, or wicked government, will you never cease to gorge on innocent victims! But let us turn away from these terrible thoughts. The army, to hinder our pursuing enemy, took the precaution (a dreadful necessity of war) of blowing up all the forts, burning all the villages, and setting fire to the corn which lay in its path. The army left Katieh on 20th Prairial [8th June]. On the 22nd it arrived at Salheyeh, where water was found. On the 23rd it reached Menzaleh and by the 24th the difference between the territory the army was now entering and the desert which it had just left began to be apparent. On the 25th we marched through the fertile fields near the Nile, and our eyes were cheered by the sight of the abundance of the crops with which they were then filled. We agreed that we had never yet seen anything more lovely.

We camped at Farescout, leaving there on the morning of 26th and arriving at Damiette after a three hour march. If our entry into the town was not brilliant, it was at least cheerful. Egypt, which we had formerly so loathed, now appeared to be a garden of delights – in comparison with Syria anyway. One did not die there either of hunger or thirst. In order to tolerate ordinariness, one must have experienced misery. I believe that Syria is to Egypt what Egypt is to France.

Having followed the adventures of the Army in Syria, it is now necessary to tell of the activities of those who had remained in Egypt. The following will accomplish this:

General Headquarters in Cairo, 1st Messidor, Year VII [19th June 1799]
Bonaparte, Commanding General, to the executive of the Directory.

Citizen Directors,
During my invasion of Syria, certain military events occurred in Lower Egypt of which I must inform you.

On 12th Pluviôse [31st January 1799] an insurrection involving part of the province of Beni-Souef took place. General Veaux[49] marched there with a battalion of the 22nd: he covered about four miles of the countryside with corpses; order was completely restored. The cost to us was three men killed and twenty wounded.

On 15th Pluviôse [3rd February] the English flotilla off Alexandria was reinforced and, shortly afterwards, began to bombard the port. The English fired fifteen or sixteen hundred shells; these caused no deaths but wrecked two wretched houses and sank a useless boat.

On 16th the flotilla left and has not reappeared.

Four gunboats left Suez on the 13th, arriving off Kosseir on 18th, where they found several buildings filled with treasure belonging to the Mameluks who had been defeated by General Desaix in Upper Egypt. After firing the first shots from its cannon the gunboat *Il Tagliamento* burst into flames and exploded. The Republic will never have any seamen until all the maritime laws are reformed. A hammock out of place, an imperfect cartridge can cause the loss of a whole squadron. Committees, assemblies, meetings must be forbidden on board ship. There must be only one voice of authority there – that of the captain – who should have even greater powers than those of Consuls in the armies of ancient Rome.

If we have had no success at sea, it is not due to the lack of capable men, or material, or money; it is caused by lack of good administration. If the organisation of the navy is allowed to continue unchanged, we might do better to close our ports for we are, at present, throwing our money into them.

Chef de Bataillon Duranteau, at the head of the 32nd, went to Charkieh on the 24th: the village of Bordein, which had rebelled, was burned and the inhabitants put to the sword.

On the 15th Ventôse [5th March], General Dugua, learning that a new tribe from the depths of Africa was arriving in the vicinity of Gizeh, ordered General Lanusse to march there, where he surprised their encampment and seized a large number of camels, having killed several hundred of their men. General Leclerc's[50] son, an outstanding young man, was wounded.

Emir Hadji, a man of weak and irresolute character on whom I have showered benefits, failed to resist the intrigues with which he was surrounded; he declared himself our enemy. Joining together with various Arab tribes and some Mameluks, he challenged us. Driven off and pursued, he lost in one day all the benefits I had bestowed on him, his treasure and part of his family, who were still in Cairo, as well as his reputation as an honest man, which he had previously enjoyed. At the beginning of Floréal [10th May 1799] a drama, the first of its kind that we have experienced, caused the province of Bahireh to rebel. A man, coming from the depths of Africa,

---

[49] Antoine Joseph Veaux (1764–1817), Baron from 1809.

[50] Pierre Leclerc d'Ostein (1741–1800); not to be confused with the better-known General Leclerc, Charles Victor Emmanuel, 1772–1802, Napoleon's brother-in-law by virtue of his marriage to Pauline Bonaparte.

disembarked at Derneh, summoned the Arabs together, and announced himself to be the angel El-Mahdy as predicted in the Koran by the Prophet. Two hundred Moghrébins arrived a few days later, as if by chance, and put themselves under his command. The angel El-Mahdy was foretold as arriving from heaven, and this impostor claimed to have descended into the desert from the sky. This man, naked as he was, made free with gold, which he had managed to hide. Each day he moistened his fingers in a jar of milk and passed them over his lips. He took no other nourishment. He went to Damanhour, where sixty men of the the nautical legion[51] had unwisely been allowed to remain, instead of being sent to the safety of El Rahmanieh. These were surprised and murdered.

Encouraged by his success, he succeeded in inflaming the imagination of his followers. He claimed that by throwing a pinch of dust onto our cannons he would prevent the powder from firing, and cause the bullets of our guns to fall down harmlessly at the feet of true believers. Many men bore witness to a hundred miracles of this nature which he performed daily.

Chef de Brigade Lefebre left El Rahmanieh with four hundred men to march against this angel, but seeing his enemies increase every moment, he realised the impossibility of reasoning with such a mob of fanatics and placed his men in a square and for a whole day killed the lunatics who threw themselves upon our guns under the influence of their delusions. It was not until nightfall, when, counting their dead (there were more than a thousand!) and wounded, they realised that God no longer performs miracles.

On the 19th Floréal [8th May], General Lanusse, who has been extremely active wherever there have been enemies to fight, reached Damanhour and put one thousand, five hundred men to the sword; only a heap of cinders now remains to show where Damanhour once stood. The angel El-Mahdy, suffering from many wounds, felt his ardour cool. He hid himself in the desert, still surrounded by his followers, for the heads of zealots cannot be penetrated by the voice of reason.

However, the nature of this uprising caused me to speed my return to Egypt. This extraordinary drama was plotted and must have taken place at the same time as the Turkish Navy – which had disembarked the army I destroyed at Acre – arrived off Alexandria. The armament of this fleet, with which the Mameluks of Upper Egypt had been supplied by means of dromedaries, allowed them now to threaten Lower Egypt, but, defeated several times by *Chef de Brigade* Estreés – a very distinguished officer – they went down to Charkieh. General Dugua ordered General Davout[52] to proceed there. On 19th Floréal he attacked Elfi Bey. A few bursts of cannon fire having killed three of Elfi's principal captains, the rest fled terrified into the desert.

---

[51] This corps was composed of sailors left without employment following the destruction of the French fleet at Aboukir.

[52] Louis Nicolas Davout (1770–1823), later Marshal of France, Duke of Auerstädt, Prince of Eckmühl, one of Napoleon's best subordinates.

An English warship and a frigate appeared at Suez on the 15th Floréal [4th May]. A cannonade started, but the English broke off the engagement when they realised that Suez was prepared to defend itself with numerous heavy guns. The two ships disappeared.

On the 10th Prairial [29th May], General Belliard[53] and *Adjudant Général* Colonel Donzelot[54] entered Kosseir and took possession of this important position. They proceeded to put it into the best possible state of defence. The occupation of Kosseir and that of Suez and El Arich completely denied entry into Egypt from the Red Sea and Syria, in the same way that the fortification of Damiette, Rosetta and Alexandria made an attack from the sea impracticable: the Republic is thus assured forever of the possession of this beautiful part of the world, whose civilisation will have so much influence on our national greatness and on the future destiny of this ancient part of the universe.

General Lanusse, having liberated the province of Bahireh, on 17th Prairial [6th June], in the village of Katz-Fournig in Charkieh, caught up with the Moghrébins and the men who had escaped from Bahireh. He killed a hundred and fifty of them and burned the village.

On 15th Prairial I reached El Arich on my return from Syria. The temperature of the desert sand reached 44 degrees while the air temperature was 34 degrees. It was necessary to cover eleven miles in a day to find a well containing a little brackish water, which tasted sulphurous and warm, but which we drank more eagerly than a bottle of fine champagne in one of our restaurants.

My entry into Cairo took place on 26th Prairial [15th June], where I was surrounded by an immense crowd who had decorated the streets, and by all the Muftis mounted on mules (for the Prophet preferred to ride these animals), all the Janissaries, the Ogeachs, the chiefs of police, the descendants of Abu-Bekr,[55] of Fatima,[56] and of many of the holy men revered by the true believers. They were led by the chief merchants and the Copt patriarch; the rear was brought up by Greek auxiliary troops.

I must make known my satisfaction with Generals Dugua and Lanusse and with *Chef de Bataillon* Duranteau. The Sheikhs El-Bekry, El-Cherkaouy, Sadât, El-Mehdy[57] and El-Saouy have behaved as well as I could have wished. They preach daily in the mosques in our favour, and their written

---

[53] Auguste Daniel Belliard (1769–1832), Count from 1810.

[54] François Xavier Donzelot (1764–1843).

[55] Abu-Bekr (c. 570–634) was chief advisor to Mohammed, who was married to Abu-Bekr's daughter, Aïsha. On the Prophet's death he was elected leader of the Muslim community and given the title 'Caliph'.

[56] The daughter of Mohammed.

[57] This is Mohammed El-Mehdy, a sheikh who was the secretary of the Government of Cairo.

orders have great influence in the provinces. They are mostly descendants of the first Caliphs and are much revered by the people.
Bonaparte.

The entry of the Commander-in-Chief into Cairo was certainly an occasion for great joy amongst the people and their leaders, who praised him constantly for his great achievements. It has to be admitted, too, that great care was taken to allow only news which was to our advantage to become known, such as, for example, that we had entirely destroyed Acre, laid waste the surroundings and killed or taken prisoner the soldiers who had defended it, that we had only quit Syria because destiny had recalled us to Egypt, etc. It is necessary to have lived among these people to understand exactly how ignorant and credulous they are. The Divans and the Sheikhs sent an address to their followers to ensure their cooperation with this great man, who, they said, read the Koran each day, and would convert to Mohammedism.

A second report, which was made to the Directory by the Commander-in-Chief, informed us of what had happened in Upper Egypt during our excursion into Syria.

General Headquarters, Cairo, 5th Messidor [23rd June 1799]

Citizens Directors,
After the Battle of the Pyramids, the Mameluks split up. Ibrahim Bey retreated into Charkieh, crossed the desert, and then remained at Gaza and Damas. Weakened by the losses he suffered during my incursion into Syria, he is now in a most miserable condition.

Murad Bey sailed up the Nile with a considerable fleet and retreated into Upper Egypt. Defeated at Sediman, he is still in control of the provinces and in a position to menace us.

On 20th Frimaire [10th December 1798], General Desaix, having been reinforced by most of the Army's cavalry, set off, arriving at Gizeh on 9th Nivôse [29th December 1798]. Two miles away, Murad Bey, who had been joined by Hassan Bey, awaited him together with two thousand Arabs of Yambo who had just disembarked at Girgeh and a considerable number of insurgent peasants. General Desaix, learning that several groups of Arabs were occupying the banks of the Nile and opposing the progress of ships carrying his munitions and supplies, despatched General Davout with the cavalry, who found and dispersed gatherings of Arabs at Sohag and Tahtah on 14th and 19th Ventôse [4th and 9th March 1799]. In these two engagements he slaughtered more than two thousand men. *Chef de Bataillon* Peron at the head of the 15th, and Boufrard at the head of the 20th Dragoons distinguished themselves particularly. Having been rejoined by his cavalry and the flotilla, Desaix marched towards the enemy, meeting them on 5th Pluviôse at the village of Samhoud. He adopted the usual order of battle, with the infantry in squares on the wings and the cavalry drawn up in a square in the centre. The right wing was commanded by General Friant,[58] the left by General Belliard and the centre by General Davout. A whirlwind of cavalry attacked our little army, but, having been stoutly repelled by a hail of bullets, they started to retreat, and our cavalry, coming into action, set off in pursuit. A hundred Arabs and peasants were slain and the rest escaped and fled into the desert.

The flag of the Republic flew above the Cataracts, all Murad Bey's fleet has been captured and, from this moment, Upper Egypt is conquered. General Desaix has stationed his division along the Nile and commenced the administration of the provinces. The remaining Mameluks and the Arabs of Yambo cannot survive in the desert. The need to obtain provisions as well as water from the Nile caused many Arabs, unable to threaten us politically, to join us, as they no longer had any artillery or ships. The only object of the battle had been pillage; but the good strategy of General Desaix and the courage of his troops had denied them even this consolation.

Chef de Brigade Courroux with the 61st was attacked at Keneh on the 22nd Pluviôse by five or six hundred Arabs, and he left the battlefield strewn with dead. General Friant marched to Samathor on 24th Pluviôse [12th February 1799], where he had been informed that the Arabs of Yambo had gathered: he killed two hundred of them. On the 23rd Pluviôse [11th February 1799], at the ruins of Thebes, two hundred men of the 22nd Régiment Chasseur and of the 15th Dragoons charged two hundred Mameluks and drove them off. They retreated into the desert leaving some of their number on the battlefield. The commander of the 22nd Lassalle conducted himself with his usual bravery.

On 17th Ventôse [7th March 1799], Murad Bey went to Esneh. Commandant Clément, an aide-de-camp of General Desaix, scattered his forces and drove them back into the desert. Learning that I had left Egypt and was crossing the desert into Syria, the Mameluks believed that General Desaix must be weakened and, from then on, sought the right moment to attack. They redoubled their efforts, hurrying from all parts of the desert to the Nile. They captured one of our *Djerms* and, murdering the crew, secured eight cannon, then, reinforced by one-thousand five-hundred men who had just debarked at Kosseir, they gathered together at Beyrouth whence they broke out. General Belliard marched against them on the 20th Nivôse [9th January 1799], attacked them, killed half of them and scattered the rest. This was the battle in which the enemy proved most stubborn.

On 13th Germinal [2nd April 1799], General Desaix, being informed that Hassan Bey planned to proceed to Keneh, marched into the desert to find him. The 7th Hussars and 8th Dragoons came upon the enemy, charged and dispersed them after a resolute battle. The Commander of the 7th Hussars was killed at the head of his regiment.

---

[58] Louis Friant (1758–1829), Count from 1808.

CHAPTER VI

On 16th Germinal [5th April 1799] *Chef de Bataillon* Morand[59], attacked in the village of Girgeh, was aided by the inhabitants, and drove off the Arabs and peasants, having killed more than a hundred men. *Chef de Brigade* Lasalle[60] marched to Theneh during the night of 20th Germinal [9th April 1799], surprised a mob he found there, killed a hundred of them and dispersed the rest. The Mameluks, finding Upper Egypt to be full of troops, made their way through the desert to Lower Egypt. General Desaix sent General Davout after them; he came up with them at the village of Bench-addy, and attacked and dispersed them, after having killed a thousand men. Three of our men were killed and thirty wounded, but among those killed was *Chef de Brigade* Simon of the 13th Dragoons, an officer of exceptional merit.

Bonaparte.

---

[59] Charles Antoine Louis Alexis Morand (1771–1835), General from 1800, Count from 1808.
[60] Antoine Charles Louis Lasalle (1775–1809), Count from 1808; one of the most dashing of French cavalry commanders, regarded as the archetypal hussar; killed at Wagram.

CHAPTER VII

LEISURE IN DAMIETTE – ZULIMA'S STORY – LIFE IN A HAREM – NEWS OF TURKISH CAPTURE OF ABOUKIR

It was from Cairo that the Commander-in-Chief sent the above dispatch to the Directory: as for us, we remained at Damiette during the month of Messidor [19th June to 18th July 1799]. We really needed this time to sort ourselves out and relax, and, although we were constantly on our guard, we had no serious problems with the enemy. I took advantage of this period of calm to study the country and its inhabitants.

I went, first, to have a massage – or rather to take a steam bath. I was led into a room shaped like a rotunda which was open at the top, so that air could enter freely; there was a platform, covered with carpet all around it. It was there that I left my clothes. When I had undressed, I placed a towel round my waist and put on some red sandals. I then went into a narrow passage where I began to feel the heat. The door closed behind me; after twenty paces another one opened in front of me. I followed a corridor which was at a right angle to the first. The bathing area was a large, vaulted room paved and panelled in marble. There were four small rooms, one at each side; steam rose continually from a fountain and from a basin in which boiling water was mixed with perfume. I at once began to sweat profusely. A slave arrived who massaged me, turning my body and manipulating my joints so that they cracked, and all without causing me the slightest discomfort. When this was over he put on a fabric glove and proceeded to rub me down for a long while; then, having led me into one of the adjoining cabinets, he poured perfumed, foaming soap over my head and left me. There were two taps in the cabinet, one of hot and one of cold water, so that I could wash myself thoroughly; then, having wrapped myself in warm linen, I followed my guide through passages leading to the outer apartment. There, on the dais I found a bed already prepared. I threw myself on it in delicious comfort.

Soon a young boy arrived, who gently patted me all over, so that I was

94

perfectly dry. I changed my clothing once more, and the boy scraped the soles and the calluses of my feet gently with pumice stone. Finally he brought me a bowl of black coffee which I was glad to drink. I gave him a few sous and he departed joyfully. I did the same after I had paid the proprietor of the baths.

It is hard to believe the pleasure one experiences in such circumstances as these. When one has been in the hot, humid mist of a steam room, where sweat pours from the body, and is then transported into a spacious apartment open to the fresh air, the lungs draw in the coolness voluptuously. The blood circulates freely and it is as if one had been relieved of a great weight. There is a feeling of suppleness, a new lightness, like being new-born and living for the first time. I returned there often, sometimes alone, sometimes with my friends.

The stay at Damiette brought me other pleasures than those of the bath, and other torments than those of war. Although I have said that the ladies of Egypt were not fit to take their place at the court of Amathonte,[61] or to capture French hearts, it should not be thought that all the women who lived in Egypt were so undeserving of the attention of travellers. It was known that the Beys, their ministers and principal officers caused the most lovely women to be brought from Georgia and the Caucasus; these they bought and raised to the rank of their wives. These ladies excelled even the most elegant in Paris or Lyon. However, they were imprisoned in harems, unseen by any men other than their husbands, and we were forbidden, on pain of death, to violate these sacred sanctuaries. The women went out only to attend communal prayer at the mosque; they were even then accompanied by old slaves who watched their every glance. I had long abandoned any thought of romance when fortune or my lucky star brought me – what shall I say – this happiness, or this misfortune. I leave it to the following narrative to decide.

I was lodged in Damiette on the street which led directly to the principal mosque, and I frequently loitered on my doorstep to watch the devout believers in the Prophet pass by. Among them I noticed one, richly dressed, who, whenever she passed me, slowed her steps and turned her eyes in my direction. I could not see her face to judge whether she was young or old, beautiful or ugly, but from her general appearance, her youthful and assured carriage, her slender and elegant form, I should not have thought her to be more than twenty years old. As for the regularity of her features, the freshness of her colouring, there I could have been mistaken. My gaze could not penetrate the double thickness of veil with which female Muslims

---

[61] Ancient city of Cyprus, celebrated for the temple of Adonis and Aphrodite.

cover their faces. I left to time and opportunity the task of enlightening me on this subject. One day, when she was, as usual, on her way to the mosque, she contrived to pass very close to me; I took the risk of saluting her, as the French salute their officers when they meet, by raising my hand to my forehead, and accompanied the salute with a warm smile. She brought her hand to her breast near her heart and, by this means, told me that she understood me. That evening after nightfall, a slave from Marseilles who was her servant asked to speak to me. I led her to my room. The first question she asked me was whether I could understand and if I could write in Arabic. I replied:

'Why do you ask?'

'My mistress, who you greeted this morning, sent me to ask the question – I have no idea why, and it is none of my business to know.'

'Who is your mistress?'

'Sir, I have been forbidden to say, I am ruined if I do not obey the orders given to me.'

'My good woman, you are French, for you speak my language.'

'Yes, sir, I come from Marseilles, I was captured by Corsairs nearly twenty years ago, and I was sold by them to an Egyptian Bey who employed me as a lady's maid for his wives.'

'Good! So, as you are French, you can confide your secret to a Frenchman; you won't be betrayed, I give you my word of honour. Who is this lady who has sent you to me?'

'Since you give me your word of honour and I trust the word of a French officer, I will tell you that she who has sent me to you is the wife of a Bey killed at the Battle of the Pyramids. Your rapid entry into Cairo did not give the Beys time to take their wives into the desert when they fled there. Some withdrew in one direction, others in another. Some of them fell into the hands of your generals who dried their tears, gave them reason to forget their husbands – or rather their tyrants – and lavished the most loving care generously upon them. My mistress, having fled from Cairo, came here to Damiette and sought refuge with a rich Turkish merchant who, to protect her from unwelcome attentions, permits it be thought that she is his wife. He shows her every mark of deference and respect. He hopes that, when Egypt has rid itself of the French, he will be able to hand her on to other Beys, who will reward him richly. But, I beg you, should you ever speak to her, do not let her know that you are aware who she is – she may, perhaps, tell you herself, but it would be better that it came from her rather than from me.'

'Do not be anxious, my dear; but what is her name? Is she young and charming?'

'Her name is Zulima, she is nineteen years old and no one more lovely

Right: Napoleon c. 1797 (engraving by Greatbatch). *Courtesy of Philip Haythornthwaite*

Below: Napoleon in Egypt (print after Meissonier). *Courtesy of Philip Haythornthwaite*

Above: The French disembark at Malta, 10th June 1798.

Left: Rear Admiral Lord Horatio Nelson, who pursues Napoleon's fleet across the Mediterranean with the aim of annihilating his enemy.

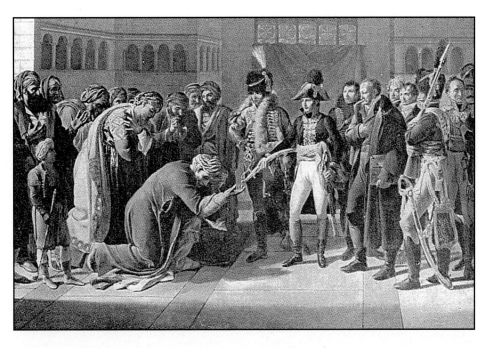

The military governor of Alexandria swears allegiance to the French cause in Egypt, following the arrival of Napoleon's army on 3rd July 1798.

Napoleon visits The Sphinx in September 1798.

An image taken from a popular print of the Battle of the Pyramids, where the French defe
Cairo. Moiret writes of the Mameluk soldiers: 'There they sat on their Arab horses ... maki
to frighten any but a French soldier'. Following the Mameluks' retreat from battle, the div

army on 21st July 1798. The two armies face each other on the bank of the Nile opposite damascene scimitars flash before our eyes. This impressive sight would have been enough , Bon and Menou proceed to the enemy camp at Embabeh and burn the village.

Rivals in Upper Egypt: General Desaix (**left**) (engraving by R. G. Tietze after Guérin; *courtesy of Philip Haythornthwaite*) and Murad Bey (**above**), leader of the Mameluk warriors.

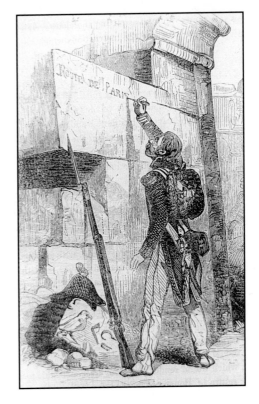

Above: Napoleon addresses the rebels in Cairo following the revolt of 21st October 1798. The interpreter stands in the centre; to the left of the picture we see Murat, dressed as a hussar.

Right: A homesick French soldier in Egypt (engraving after Horace Vernet). *Courtesy of Philip Haythornthwaite*

Left: General Lannes, injured at the two-month siege of St Jean-d'Acre, 1799 (engraving by Kruell after Guérin). *Courtesy of Philip Haythornthwaite*

Below: French forces fail to win Acre, and Napoleon recalls the Army of Syria to Egypt on 17th May 1799. The return journey across the desert is beset by plague, injury and terrible thirst.

Above: 'A lively cannonade' from the first land battle of Aboukir is heard by Moiret and his compatriots at dawn on 24th July 1799. By the time they arrive eight days later, the French are triumphant against the Turks.

Left: Murat leads a successful charge at Aboukir and is promoted to General of Division on the battlefield. He is wounded in the jaw and shortly after returns to France with Bonaparte (engraving by Bosselman). *Courtesy of Philip Haythornthwaite*

General Berthier (**left**) (engraving by H. Davidson after Gros) and (**below**) aide-de-camp de Beauharnais (print after Albrecht Adam), two members of the elite chosen to accompany Napoleon to France in August 1799, following news of French reverses in Europe.
Courtesy of Philip Haythornthwaite

Portrait of General Kléber (engraving by T. Johnson after Guérin; *courtesy of Philip Haythornthwaite*); and (**below**) in battle. Shortly after victory at Aboukir, Napoleon abandons the Army of the Orient, leaving Kléber in command. Kléber 'arrives too late' at Rosetta to discuss his appointment with Bonaparte.

General Menou (**left**) succeeds Kléber to command following the latter's assassination on 14th June 1800. A convert to Islam, Menou is less popular with the French soldiers, and also encounters dissent from his subordinate generals, including General Reynier (**below**) (print after Guérin; *courtesy of Philip Haythornthwaite*), whom he has arrested and despatched to France in March 1801.

British generals Abercromby (**right**) (mortally wounded at the Second Battle of Aboukir, 22nd March 1801) and (**below**) his successor John Hely Hutchinson. (Engravings by J. Chapman.)

The Death of Abercromby (print c. 1818).

Above: Napoleon as First Consul c.1801 (engraving by Meret after Appiani), and (**left**) Admiral Sir Sidney Smith (engraving by Greatbatch after Robert Ker Porter), who fought against him during the defence of Acre. Napoleon said of Smith: '[He] is a brave officer ... active, intelligent, intriguing and indefatigable, but I believe he is half mad'. *Courtesy of Philip Haythornthwaite*

has ever been seen, not even at Aix, which is famed for female beauty. But, Captain, tell me, what answer shall I take her?'

'Tell her that in the year I have been in Egypt, I have learned to speak Arabic like a native, and that I am at her service, if I should be so fortunate as to please her.'

'I shall tell her that without fail', she said.

In order to get her on my side, I gave her some coins, and she left.

As surprised as delighted by this turn of events, which would have seemed improper for a woman in France, I dreamed all night about this budding intrigue. On the one hand I feared to involve myself. I thought, 'What sorrows are you preparing for yourself! Your heart will no sooner be engaged than your superiors will order you to Cairo or Alexandria and you will leave a wretched lover behind you in misery'. On the other hand I longed to love and to be loved. What should I do? If the colony should flourish and become established in the country, I should have a wife all ready for me, who would bring me happiness and fortune as a dowry. Troubled by these various thoughts I slept but little, and finally made up my mind to continue with the adventure.

On the following day I received, from the same messenger, the following letter, written in Arabic.

> Young and gallant Frenchman,
> I have made an approach to you which, in your own country, would have led you to think ill of me: but you would be wrong to judge me by the prejudice of your nation. Remember that my heart is untried and that you are the first to master and conquer it. Your soldierly air, handsome appearance and your frank and open manners have overwhelmed me; so, I must confess, I love you. If you do not spurn my passion, try to obtain an invitation from the merchant with whom I reside. Love will do the rest.
> Your friend,
> *Zulima*.

This proposal, far from being displeasing, gave me great satisfaction. The French are as swift in love as in courage; they do not like to delay, sighing, like the Italians and Spanish for years together beneath the balcony of some beauty. It was a simple matter for me to gain admittance to the merchant's house; my rank as a staff officer entitled me to a certain respect. I led him to hope to supply the sheets and fabrics which my corps might need. From the very first meeting with him I won his confidence – even his friendship. There I found Zulima at his side, for she was not kept in the solitude of the harem like the merchant's wives. On that day her face was covered only by the outer veil, which was transparent enough for one to be able to distinguish her features; then I could see that she was as her slave had described her. When the merchant turned away to select some fabrics for me to choose

113

from, she drew her veil slightly aside, showing me features and colouring such as might pierce a heart of iron. I wafted a kiss to her and, with her hand, she returned one to me. I did not hope, that day, to be able to go further. I wished to know the merchant better, and to await other more favourable opportunities. I ordered some yards of fabric, paid and left, taking leave of the merchant and his protégée. I returned two days later under the pretext of purchasing some more goods. Imagine my astonishment when Aboulferu (that was the merchant's name) begged me to be so kind as to come and give lessons in mathematics and French grammar to Zulima!

'My clerks are all Copts and Greeks', he told me, 'and they lie to me and rob me. Zulima, who I look upon as a daughter and who has a charming nature, will quickly learn whatever you teach her, and I shall then put her in charge of my account books and of my correspondence with French merchants. As for me, if I can be of service to you in any way you may count upon my help as well as upon my gratitude.'

It may be imagined how gladly I accepted the offer he made me, unexpected though it was; Zulima had certainly arranged it. I declared myself ready to begin my duties at once, and to this he agreed. I was shown into a room next to the shop, and the lovely Zulima was brought in for her first lesson.

I shall not attempt to describe my emotions at this, my first clear sight of one whom I had previously seen only as if through a cloud, nor can I describe how I expressed my gratitude and tenderness. In these first few moments, we only stammered some disconnected phrases which barely expressed our feelings. On that occasion I instructed her in certain principles of numeration and addition, both of us in a state of distraction due to our mutual confusion. Some time later, the merchant being absent, we talked more freely of our love, and of her history which she told me thus:

'I was born near Tiflis in Georgia. The overlord of our village, wishing to raise money with which to buy himself a wife, as is the custom in that country, sold me with several of my companions to an Armenian merchant. I was then fourteen years old. I was taken first to Constantinople, but, as I did not have the plump body the Turks prefer, the price offered for me was not as high as was demanded by the merchant; not as high, in fact, as what I had cost him. He decided to bring me to Cairo to sell. I was bought by Ali Bey, who was slain on the battlefield of the Pyramids. When you French entered Cairo I fled and came here to Damiette to the home of Aboulferu, who had been an intimate friend of Ali Bey.'

At this point I interrupted Zulima to ask her if she had not mourned the death of her husband, had not shed tears at his fate, did not hate the French who had caused his untimely end.

'My husband!' she returned sharply, 'No, no, I never experienced the sweetness of marriage with him. I told you already that the Muslims love only great masses of flesh. He who you call my husband – who I look upon only as a tyrant – was waiting for me to attain the desired bulk before "honouring" me with his attention. In any case, weary and sated with the love of women, this monster gave himself over to unnatural pleasures and spurned normal delights. Men such as this keep women in their harems only as luxuries: there is none of the sensitivity, the consideration, the delicacy which, in Europe, always accompanies true affection. Nevertheless, he did have one favourite, whom he appointed to have absolute authority over us, and who made us aware of this all the time. Oppressed by this shrew, watched over by base creatures who spied on our every word, look and movement, how could we be happy? How could we regret a master to whom we were bound only by fear and dread? As the French had rendered me the service of eliminating a tyrant, I shall feel eternal gratitude to them.'

'I very much wish to know', I said, 'What life is like in these hidden places called harems, where even we, the conquerors of Egypt, are forbidden to enter.'

'I was aware', she replied, 'that women played a brilliant part in European society. Here, we were humiliated and enslaved, confined to an inner room where we had no company but that of our aged slaves. We never met men, not even at meals. Should our master wish to dine with one of his wives, he had her so informed, then she would perfume her rooms with costly essences, prepare the most delicate foods, receive her lord, tremblingly, and show him the most seductive attentions. When we were alone we spent our time embroidering sashes, making veils and at the spinning wheel. We pretended a gaiety that we did not feel, we sung tender airs, or the praises of our master and our voices were accompanied by the tambourines and castanets of the slaves. Entertainers came sometimes to cheer us with their dances and pretty voices and to tell romantic tales. A dainty meal of delicious flavours and exquisite fruits ended the day. Sometimes we were allowed out into the fresh air on the flat roof of the palace, but, to prevent the men who call from the top of the minarets from seeing us, they were compelled to swear to close their eyes as they announced the times of prayer. This precaution was taken even further and usually only blind men were chosen to carry out this holy duty.

'Sometimes we went out, under the guard of black eunuchs, for a trip on the Nile. Our barges, richly decorated, were beautifully carved and exquisitely painted. They could be identified by the blinds which were lowered over the windows and by the music which played on board. These were the pleasures we enjoyed together; but they did not equal the sufferings which we had to undergo without a murmur of complaint. Jealousy, suspicion, false accusations, insulting reprimands and abusive sarcasm

115

made life in the harem worse than hell. To stop the quarrels of these vulgar women, or to punish imaginary misdeeds whispered into the ear of the master by his favourite, we were beaten with canes and sometimes death was the result. A Circassian, one of my companions, on her way to the mosque one day, had the misfortune to turn her head towards a European who was chatting nearby; this was duly reported to the Bey by an accursed slave. The tyrant, enraged, dragged the miserable girl by her hair from our midst into the courtyard and cut off her head with a single blow of his sabre. How could you expect us, gentle Frenchman, to love such oppressors, or to shed tears on their graves, when death delivers us from them! Ah! I beg you, young lover, beloved soldier, take me away from this loathsome country, take me with you to France should your fate recall you there!'

The tears which she could not help shedding at these words rendered her even more lovely. Touched by her sad fate and very moved, I promised her to do everything I could to rescue her from the miseries which awaited her in Egypt if the French should leave the country and I added:

'Dare I hope, my Zulima, to see my love rewarded soon, in return for the vows I make you?'

'Alas', she returned, 'I dare not trust your vows unless they are consecrated under the seal of religion and law. I know of the unfaithfulness of the French, how their passion, quickly aroused, may vanish as soon as satisfied. Their affections, like their fashions, change from one day to the next.'

'Believe me, Madame, that I am one of those who are an exception to the rule. You wish me to make our union legal in the eyes of religion – but what religion is it to be? For you must not expect me to become a Muslim, to muffle my head in a turban, and undergo that humiliating operation which distinguishes the Jew and the Muslim, to forswear for ever that strengthening liquor invented by Noah. I shall never follow in the footsteps of our General Abdallah,[62] who has scandalised the entire Army. I should be the object of the jests of all my comrades. There are prejudices – if prejudices they are – which should be respected, and how could you expect me to be faithful to the vows I make to you if I should be unfaithful to those which bind me to the religion in which I was born and brought up?'

'Ah! Cruel one', she said with feeling, 'Do you wish me to abandon mine! Even should I wish it, how could I do so without putting myself in danger? Aboulferu, who has sheltered me, is, like all other Turks, entirely devoted to Islam. There is, for him, no law but that of Mohammed; in order to defend it he would be prepared to sacrifice his own life. If he should see me become a Christian, he would be capable of having you entrapped and

---

[62] General Menou, who had converted to Islam under the name of Abdallah.

murdered upon the dying body of your beloved.

'You could never imagine to what excesses their fanaticism will lead the true believers. In their eyes, Christians are cursed of God followed everywhere by misfortune, doomed to failure in all things.'

'Then, Madam', I rejoined, 'We must bid each other an eternal farewell. I assure you that this separation will cause me pain, but it seems to me that too many obstacles stand in the way of our happiness should we continue to meet.'

I spoke thus for I felt sure that she would not consent so soon to end a love affair which had hardly begun.

'To overcome these difficulties', she replied, 'When you leave for France, let me know. I will follow you with my wealth and my jewels. There, before your altar, you will give me your hand; your God will be mine, your laws, mine also. I shall revere your parents above my own who repudiated me. I shall become your wife, your queen, while here I am nothing but a slave. There I shall have no rival, I alone will possess your heart.'

I took her hand, and kissed it lovingly to seal the pact. I continued to see her as often as I could, and to give her lessons in arithmetic and grammar. She was a good pupil, having an excellent memory and reliable judgement, as well as the most agreeable disposition. I spent the happiest hours during my stay at Damiette in conversation with her, listening to the outpourings of her heart. We agreed to write to each other frequently, should I be forced to leave Damiette with my corps, either for Cairo or elsewhere; I promised her faithfully that I would let her know if we were about to return to France, so that she might escape and join me, together with her loyal servant. What actually happened we shall see in due course.

The separation which I had foreseen and dreaded took place sooner than I could have wished. For it was on the 19th July 1799 that we received the order to leave Damiette immediately; no reason for the move was given to us.

Most of us thought that it was to escape new dangers; moreover, there was a rumour going around that there would be a landing on the Mediterranean coast which could result in dire consequences for us and for the colony. It was not until we reached El Rahmanieh that we were told bluntly that the troops of the Grand Turk had disembarked at Aboukir, slaughtered the garrison and made themselves masters of the fortification. Disastrous Aboukir, loathsome port, are you doomed always to witness our catastrophes and misfortunes? Are you not sickened at the awful sight of our devastated fleet? Do you wish to rejoice again at the sight of us murdered or loaded with chains? Ah! Let us march onwards to avoid such shame if we can: orders were arriving continually, urging us to hasten forward.

117

CHAPTER VIII

'UTTER DEFEAT' OF TURKISH ARMY – PURSUIT OF MURAD BEY – ENG-
LISH COME ASHORE AT KOSSEIR – BONAPARTE THREATENS DIVAN –
NEWS OF FRENCH REVERSES IN ITALY AND ON THE RHINE – BONAPARTE
LEAVES IN SECRET FOR FRANCE – KLÉBER'S FIRST PROCLAMATION AS
COMMANDER-IN-CHIEF – ARMIES OF THE GRAND VIZIER AND DJEZZAR
PASHA UNITE AGAINST THE FRENCH – NEGOTIATIONS WITH SIR SIDNEY
SMITH AND THE GRAND VIZIER – LOSS OF EL ARICH – AGREEMENT TO
EVACUATE EGYPT

From daybreak on the 6th Thermidor [24th July 1799], we heard the
incessant noise of a lively cannonade. Courage and enthusiasm were not
wanting, but physical strength was lacking. The soldiers were falling from
exhaustion, hunger and thirst. Mercifully, we were told that the enemy was
beaten, that they had been cleared from the fortifications, that they had
thrown themselves headlong into the sea, hoping that their fleet would save
them; our cavalry had charged them vigorously, and bullets had been
rained upon them by combined artillery and musket fire. We heard that
practically all of them had perished in the sea, and that no more than five
hundred men now remained, surrounded in a fort. We had no share in the
glory of this day, except the fatigue of a forced march. With this good news
I returned to Damiette and to Zulima, who was overjoyed to see me again.

I arrived there on the 15th of the month (Thermidor) [2 August 1799],
having spent seven days on the way. There we were told of the utter defeat
of the Turkish army, which had consisted of five thousand men, of whom
two hundred were prisoners, including their general, Mustapha Pasha, and
several other officers. This victory was bought at the price of much French
blood; we suffered a large number of wounded, amongst whom were
General Murat, *Chef de Brigade* Cretin of the engineers, and the aide-de-
camp, Guibert. The latter two died of their wounds. But here is the account
that our General gave of this great feat of arms – which I did not myself
witness.

118

Bonaparte, Commanding General

The name of Aboukir was dreadful to the French; but the seventh day of Thermidor has rendered it glorious. The victory just won by the army will expedite its return to Europe.

We conquered Mainz and the banks of the Rhine, by invading part of Germany; but today we have reconquered our settlements in the Indies and those of our allies. By one single operation we have given our government the power to compel England, despite her triumphs at sea, to conclude a peace treaty which will be glorious for the Republic.

We have suffered greatly, we have had to struggle against every sort of enemy, we have yet more to overcome, but the outcome will be worthy of us, we shall deserve the gratitude of our country.

Bonaparte.

On 21st Thermidor [8th August 1799] General Desaix learned that Murad Bey, having left the desert above Siout, had reached Elganaium. He immediately sent *Chef de Brigade* Morand in pursuit, who quickly found, attacked and beat him. Several Mameluks were killed, and a *kachef*[63] and forty camels were captured. Murad Bey retreated hurriedly, but *Chef de Brigade* Morand and his intrepid column, having covered fifty miles of desert in four days, came up with him again near Samalout on night of the 24th, surprised his camp, put a number of Mameluks to the sword and seized two hundred camels laden with booty, eleven hundred horses with their harness and an enormous quantity of arms of all types. Murad himself, fleeing from a detachment of the 20th Dragoons, only escaped under cover of night.

On the 27th Thermidor [14th August], at noon, two English frigates moored off the port of Kosseir and fired their cannon. Four hours later twelve sloops were launched intending to land troops, but these soon returned when our soldiers were seen in the village. The frigates continued their bombardment throughout the night. On the morning of the 28th, the ships changed their position to give the fort a pounding, while, at the same time, two hundred men came ashore at the village where they had not dared to disembark on the previous night. The light infantry of the 21st, who were lying in ambush, allowed the English to advance a little and then attacked them with such ferocious firepower that, in their flight, they abandoned their dead and wounded. Meanwhile, the enemy continued to pound away and in the afternoon a new attack was mounted on a large beach to the south of the port. General Donzelot, in command at Kosseir, who

---

[63] *Kachef* (also *Kashif*) is a rank similar to, but below, that of *Emir* in the Arab hierarchy. In his *Chronicle*, Al-Jabarti says that a *Kashif* is a 'sub-provincial governor'.

was directing the defence, had troops concealed in tombs bordering the sea and in ravines near the desert, so that the enemy coming under fire both on their front and flank were obliged to re-embark as quickly as they had done in the morning. Yet the cannonade from the frigates did not lessen at all, and on the 29th at 7 o'clock in the morning, four hundred men brought a six-pounder cannon ashore, together with its ammunition etc. Then we attacked the gun, which was abandoned as everyone fled in great disorder before our bayonets to regain their floating strongholds. Finally, after an uninterrupted bombardment lasting sixty-four hours, the enemy frigates cast off, set sail and vanished. Six thousand cannonballs were gathered up on the port – with calibres from 24 down to 8: no one came to claim them so we used them ourselves later on.

Amongst the troops who had disembarked were many *Cipayes*.[64] This proved that the English never fought us unless they could place others in front of them to receive our blows. The natives of the country behaved at this time like true friends, leaving no doubt of their sincere aversion to the English.

Near Damiette, to which we returned, we were resting once more as cheerfully as usual, when, on 27th Thermidor, the General told us of the presence of a fleet at the mouth of the Nile. We were too few in number to confront them successfully, and haste was made to come to our assistance. The enemy perhaps perceived this and moved off. This attempt was part of a wider plan, and should have taken place at the same time as the attack on Aboukir, with the landing of numbers of troops to engage us at various points. It appeared that conditions had kept this fleet at sea longer than intended, and this was why the attack it made did not coincide with that upon Aboukir, so we got off with a fright.

Victor at Aboukir, the Commanding General hurried back to Cairo, to make his report to the administration. It was there that he held a public meeting with the members of the government, of which I shall give an account. Having asked them various questions about art and science, which they believed to be contained in the Koran, he ended by reproaching them for the lack of enthusiasm they had shown in checking, during his absence, the grumbles which had arisen against him and his army. He told them that he was aware of the hopes they had for his failure, and that, in consequence, he had commanded that all their heads should be cut off if he had been beaten. 'How could you doubt my success?', he added. 'I told you that I should succeed before I left and that should have been enough for you. I knew God's plans for me so well that, of the ten thousand men I led to

---

[64] *Cipayes:* Indian soldiers. The origin of this word is variously traced to Portuguese and Persian sources, and it is the equivalent of the English term 'sepoy'.

Aboukir, I used only three thousand and that was enough to beat and to slay the infidels.'

After speaking for some time, he was interrupted by a member of the Divan, who said, 'General, you promised us that you would become a Muslim.'

'I did not promise you anything', he replied. 'Nevertheless, know that I am one, and, perhaps, a better one than you, and if you do not mend your ways, I shall again become a Christian to punish you. I shall overlook this, but don't forget that it is for the last time!'

On his way back to Cairo from Aboukir, Bonaparte visited Alexandria. There he learned from negotiators on English ships about the first reverses to be suffered by our armies on the Rhine and in Italy. It was not difficult for him to believe this news, for the manner in which France was governed – by five incompetent Directors, disunited amongst themselves, and two Chambers where the divergence of opinion nourished discord – could not fail to produce such results. His friends, left behind in France, urged him to return to crush the factions and himself take over the government. The *Abbé* Sieyès, our ambassador in Berlin, had obtained passports for him from that court and sent them to him secretly. The English knew about this and covertly favoured the plan. I understood from General Joubert, whom I knew well, that he had already been offered the government by members of the Directory; that he had told them that he could not accept at that time, his name not being sufficiently illustrious to draw the nation together; and that they should just give him command of the Army of Italy, then, when he had won some major victories, he would be their man.

Destiny decided otherwise at Novi,[65] as everyone knows. It was Napoleon who was chosen by destiny. Napoleon confided his secret to no one but General Berthier. Already determined on a return to Europe, he made his preparations secretly without the Army having the slightest suspicion of them. He ordered Admiral Ganteaume[66] to have ready two frigates with an escort vessel and a tartan[67] without disclosing the destination of the ships. The honour of accompanying him was granted only to Generals Lannes, Marmont,[68] Murat and Andréossy,[69] and to the scholars Monge and Berthollet,[70] to *Chef de Brigade* Rossières and to his Guides,[71] to whom

---

[65] Barthélemy Catherine Joubert (1769–1799) was killed at Novi during the Italian campaign.

[66] Honoré Joseph Antoine Ganteaume (1755–1818), Count from 1810.

[67] A small Mediterranean vessel with a large sail.

[68] Jean Lannes (1769–1809) (see Short Biographies); Auguste Frédéric Louis Viesse de Marmont (1774–1852), later Marshal of France, Duke of Raguse.

[69] Antoine François Andréossy (1761–1828), Count from 1809 (see also Appendix 2).

[70] Claude Louis Berthollet (1748–1822) (see also Appendix 2).

[71] An elite cavalry escort included in Bonaparte's bodyguard.

were given sealed orders which were not to be opened until 5th Fructidor [22nd August 1799] at such an hour and such a place on the coast. There they found instructions to embark immediately, without informing anyone. A similar packet, not to be opened until twenty-four hours after the departure of the ships, was sent to General Kléber. This enclosed his appointment as Commander-in-Chief and the appointment of Desaix to the command of Upper Egypt. In order the better to conceal his real intentions, Bonaparte gave out the false information that he was about to inspect the various regions and fortifications in Egypt. He announced that he was about to set up his headquarters at Menouf and instructed that dispatches should be sent to him there.

A few days later he changed this to Rosetta, to which he summoned General Kléber. However the General arrived too late – or rather Bonaparte left too early. Whichever it was, General Kléber found there a packet of instructions which had been left for him, and so learned that Bonaparte had left for France on the night of 6th–7th Fructidor [23rd–24th August].

This news did not cause the sensation that the reader might suppose. The Army heard the news with pleasure; they hoped soon to be recalled to France through the mediation of their leader. At the time of his departure he [Napoleon] had sent the scholars – with their eye glasses – to Upper Egypt, to discover antiquities. By this means he thought he would hide his activities from their too penetrating observation. The impatience with which we awaited our General's farewells was satisfied by the following proclamation:

Bonaparte, Commanding General of the Army

Soldiers,
The news from Europe has caused me to decide to leave for France. I leave the command of the Army to General Kléber. You will receive news from me soon, I cannot say more. I am grieved to leave the soldiers to whom I am most attached, but it will not be for long. The general I leave in charge has my confidence and that of the Government.
Bonaparte.

This is what he wrote at the same time to the Divan in Cairo.

Headquarters, Alexandria, 5th Fructidor, Year VII [22nd August 1799] from Bonaparte, Commanding General and member of the National Institute

In the name of God, clement and merciful, to the Divan of Cairo, chosen from amongst the wisest and most enlightened.

Having been informed that my squadron is ready and a formidable army embarked thereupon, convinced, as I have often told you, that, as long as I have not dealt the blow which will crush all my enemies at once, I cannot

enjoy the tranquillity of Egypt, fairest country of the earth, I have decided to place myself at the head of my squadron, leaving the command, during my absence, to General Kléber who is a distinguished soldier and whom I have advised that he should show the same friendship to the sheikhs and religious leaders that I have shown. Do all you can to ensure that the people of Egypt should have the same confidence in him that they have had in me, so that, on my return, which will be in two or three months, I shall be satisfied with the people and shall have only praise and rewards for the sheikhs.
Bonaparte.

One may think what one likes about the truthfulness of such language, but at least the first impression it made on an ignorant and credulous population prevented a sudden uprising and gave the new general time to get his bearings and take precautions. The first act of Kléber's command was to issue the following proclamation:

From the Cairo Headquarters of Commanding General Kléber, 14th Fructidor [31st August 1799]

Soldiers,
There were compelling reasons which obliged the Commander-in-Chief, Bonaparte, to return to France. Even the dangers of a voyage undertaken at a bad time of year, across a narrow sea infested with his enemies could not hold him back; it was for your well-being.

Soldiers, powerful help is on its way to us, or, perhaps, a glorious peace, a peace worthy of you and your deeds, will return you to your fatherland.

On taking up the burden which Bonaparte bore, I was aware of its importance, and of its difficulty but, on the other hand, appreciating your valour, which has so often been crowned with brilliant success, your endless patience in bearing troubles and overcoming privations. I realised, after all, that with such soldiers, anything might be attempted and achieved, so then I thought only of the advantages of leading you, of the honour of commanding you, and my confidence increased.

Soldiers, have no doubt, your pressing needs will receive my most immediate care.
Kléber.

We were not displeased to see the command pass into General Kléber's hands; the reputation for bravery which he had won when in the Army of the Rhine, the prudence he had always shown, above all at St Jean-d'Acre, his impartial sense of justice and his attractive and affable manner soon won him the army's confidence. His known character, rather different from that of his predecessor, led us to hope that he would negotiate with our enemies and might succeed in returning us to our own country. Bonaparte never did anything except in his own interest, and saw only the path leading to the advancement of his own fortune. Kléber never considered himself, his thoughts were all for the comfort and relief of the soldier; he expected promotion only on merit, and did not push himself forward. If Napoleon had not seen the opportunity to seize supreme power in his adopted country,[72] he would have remained in Egypt, where he would have created an independent state, but at the cost of all our blood. Like Caesar, he would prefer to be first in Cairo rather than second in Paris. Kléber, free of ambition, was content with the rank that fortune and his military talent had brought him; he had no personal interest in keeping us in a country where, his wisdom told him, we could never put down our roots; we had good reason to have the fairest hopes of him.

Let us look now at the direction given to affairs by this general, up to the moment when a dreadful death snatched him from our affections.

The 75th Demi-Brigade, to which I was attached, received orders to go to Cairo, so we left Damiette on the 27th Fructidor, VIIth Year [13th September 1799] and arrived at the capital three days later. There, anxious to obtain news, we were told of the new dangers menacing us. The Grand Vizier in person, together with the notorious and terrible Djezzar, Pasha of Acre, were advancing through Syria with a large and formidable army, composed of infantry, cavalry and artillery, and he had sworn utterly to exterminate us. Most of our troops were sent to the frontiers, to confront the invasion and to stem, if possible, its destructive tide.

Meanwhile, there was the matter of reaching an agreement and peace. We saw the coming and going of negotiators on both sides, as discord about terms resulted in innumerable messages being passed between them, all of which revived and reinforced our longing to return to Europe. But the real intention of the enemy was to distract us – or rather to lull us to sleep – for during these fake negotiations, a disembarkation was attempted and three or four thousand troops were landed near Damiette. We prevented any further landings.

On the 10th Brumaire [1st November 1799], a battle began which was fought stubbornly by both sides. Our soldiers, in order to settle matters quickly, had recourse to their favourite weapon. Terror went before them and cast into the flood all those the bayonets could not reach. Only about eight hundred men were left, and these were taken prisoner; among them was an Aga of the Janissaries.[73] This victory cost us a hundred men of whom thirty were killed, including, among others, the gallant Dunoyer, Commanding Officer of the 2nd Light Infantry.

The movement of the land army, under the command of the Grand

---

[72] Napoleon was a Corsican by birth.

[73] Turkish infantry: the Janissaries were forcibly recruited from the European provinces of the Ottoman and formed the elite of the Ottoman forces.

Vizier, led us to suppose that we should soon have to confront him. We were making our preparations for this when we learned that, in accordance with new proposals which our General had made to him, he had withdrawn his advance guard, which was already near the fort at El Arich. Uncertain of being able to beat us in an open and honest war, the English still sought to throw the apple of discord amongst us. Profiting from the discontent which arose from the fact that we had had no pay for seven months, Smith's[74] agents circulated documents in our ranks which insulted our leaders, the aim of which was to foment rebellion and disorder. The writers of these documents inspired our malcontents to demand an immediate return to France at any price and under any conditions. However, these murmurings did not have quite the success which those who had connived at them had hoped. The Light Infantry Demi-Brigade was practically the only one to lend an ear to these seductive voices; the 3rd, 14th and 2nd[75] Dragoons Regiments and the 32nd of the line were not entirely above reproach in this matter. By an order of the 9th Frimaire, Year VIII [29th November 1799], the 2nd Light Infantry was disbanded and the personnel incorporated in other corps whose conduct had remained unexceptionable.

On the 17th of the same month, the Commanding General called together all the officers of the Cairo garrison and, after having assured them that he had done all in his power for the well-being of the army and explained the army's financial situation, its receipts and expenses, he urged them to take steps to prevent such disorder as had compelled him to act harshly in the case of the 2nd Light Infantry. This action, he told them, had pained him to the heart, but a stern example had to be made. He added that he was quite determined to disband any corps which behaved in that way. He told them also of the point his negotiations with the Grand Vizier had reached; [he told them] that he would avoid battle as far as was possible, but if, having tried all other means, this was the only option, he would take it, would win, and was sure that they and their men would back him up. He said, too, that he would do everything he possibly could to ensure that they would return to France in the summer, but that if it meant the sacrifice of his honour and the glory of his army, even if he was alone, he would have no part of it. His audience were impressed by this frank disclosure of his thoughts and actions, and promised him their loyalty and support.

Soon afterwards he sent General Desaix and M. Poussielgue[76] to the

---

[74] Commodore Sir Sidney Smith, Commander of the British Squadron at sea (see Short Biographies).

[75] It seems likely that Captain Moiret was mistaken as the 2nd Dragoons were not in Egypt. The reference may be to the 20th Dragoons, who were present at the time.

[76] Jean-Baptiste Poussielgue (1764–1845) (see also Appendix 2).

English Commodore (on board the *Tigre*) to convey his final views on peace or war. It seemed that the Grand Vizier would act only in accordance with English policies and these did not appear to favour us, so we were compelled to make ready for renewed battles. General Kléber wished first to reorganise the 2nd Light Infantry which he had disbanded. He had punished them regretfully; it was through justice and goodness of character that he pardoned them, in order that a majority of innocent persons should not be condemned with the handful of guilty ones who they had, moreover, already denounced. The whole army was grateful to this good general and let him know it.

Our negotiators, having failed to find the *Tigre* at the appointed rendezvous, took its disappearance as a refusal to treat and an intention to break off discussions. As a result we left Cairo on the 9th Nivôse [30th December 1799] and set out to meet the enemy. We arrived at Belbeiss on the 10th, where we were informed that a gust of wind had driven the English admiral off-shore and that negotiations had been re-started. So, we were ordered to return to Cairo! At our first halt at Bellotte, General Reynier, commanding the advance guard, turned us round, announcing that the enemy was moving. Back again at Belbeiss we were informed of the conclusion of a truce for one month: this news made us think that General Reynier had been misled, all the more so as he wrote to the Commanding General that he had been mistaken! Our uncertainty ended on the 14th, the day on which we learned of the loss of El Arich. It was said that this loss was due to the dissension which was spread among the troops defending the fort. Blind to their own interests, several individuals sent a petition to the Commander to give the place up; it was even believed that traitors had pulled enemy soldiers into the fort with ropes. These people then helped themselves to whatever they came across. But others of the French, undoubtedly disagreeing with the former, set fire to the powder-store. The explosion killed many of our troops, as well as the enemy. They say, also, that prisoners-of-war imprisoned in the fort opened a gate to let the Turks in; this took place at the moment when the signed capitulation was about to go into effect. The loss, which deprived us of nearly four hundred men and facilitated the entry of the enemy into Egypt, was enough to alarm us and to presage one of our bloodiest battles. Something had to be done. Therefore, we left Belbeis on the 15th and spent the night at Koraïm. On the 16th we reached Salheyeh, where the army was gathering. The news of the truce had not reached the Grand Vizier until after the capture of El Arich, and so it was also there that he suspended his activities until the expiration of the time agreed upon.

The Commanding General reached Salheyeh on 22nd Nivôse [11th January] and, having called together the officers who had reported to him, he told them that General Bonaparte, before his departure, had begun negotiations with the Grand Vizier. 'Negotiations', he said, 'which I have continued up to the present moment. His only intention was to return you to France, but I am unable to agree to the proposals made to me. I believe that there is not one soldier who would not prefer death to laying down his arms. Would anyone wish to return to his native land, naked, robbed of everything, like a vagabond, chased from a country where he had once made himself feared? Moreover, can we know to what fate we would be condemned, once we were defenceless? No. We must fight again and win; victorious, we shall be able to dictate conditions and negotiate with honour. Our fellow countrymen must see us arrive with our tattered flags, our arms on our shoulders and with the warlike music of drums going before us. Watching us, they will say, "Behold these heroes, betrayed by fortune, but never abandoned by victory: behold the terrible 32nd, the invincible 75th, etc. returning from the Orient with those flags which they so bravely defended on the banks of the Po, the Piave and the Rhine." Promise me victory and I will promise you a glorious return to France. If we are beaten I can guarantee neither your honour nor your life. Our safety depends upon our courage.'

This speech, whose emotion I can only imperfectly reproduce, convinced us of the inevitability and the necessity of a further battle, and made us the more impatient for it as our return to France, goal of our most fervent longings, would be assured by success.

Meanwhile, General Kléber continued, through General Desaix, to negotiate with the Grand Vizier, Commodore Sidney Smith and the Russian Commissioner. Whenever we saw a courier arrive from the negotiators we imagined that he carried the signal to start hostilities, and rushed spontaneously to our posts. After a few days we learned that peace was almost agreed, and then that the treaty had been concluded; when work on the fortifications was stopped we decided that the news was true. The Commanding General ended our uncertainty with the following:

At Salheyeh Camp, 8th Pluviôse, Year VIII [28th January 1800]
Kléber, Commanding General of the Army

Soldiers,
A series of circumstances, of which I am still unable to inform you, has decided me to halt our victories and to negotiate with our enemies rather than fight them. Thus, as a result of the treaty which I have just concluded, you will, in four months time, again see your fatherland, where you will be able to put your arms and your valour to greater use than you could do in this country.

Soldiers, if I had been consulted about the burden handed to me by General Bonaparte, I most certainly would not have accepted it, for I was only too well aware that I was unequal to the importance of the post I occupy under circumstances so difficult: but, as you know, I had no option. However, I have the consolation of knowing that, though I may not have been able to do for you all that your courage and devotion to the Republic merits, at least I have done all that it was humanly possible to do under the difficult circumstances in which the army is placed. Those of you who are not deaf to the voice of reason will do me the justice of believing what I say. I care little what others may think.[77]

Soldiers, mutual commitments bind you and the Ottoman Army; I am convinced that neither the Grand Vizier nor any of his Muslim commanders has any intention of betraying these commitments but, given their dissolute institutions, are they able, always, to answer for the conduct of their subordinates? Certainly not. It will be up to you with your good and sensible discipline to avoid and prevent those brawls which would cause enormous trouble and have dire results. I will not leave unpunished a single insult offered to you, but, also, I shall punish, with the utmost rigor of the law, any among you who might have provoked them.
Kléber.

The 'mutual commitments' binding the French Army to the Ottoman Army to which Kléber referred in his address, were contained in the following agreement signed at El Arich on 4th Pluviôse of the same year [24th January 1800].

AGREEMENT

For the Evacuation of Egypt, reached between Citizens Desaix, General of Division, and Poussielgue, Financial Administrator and Plenipotentiary of the Commanding General, and their Excellencies Mustapha-Rachid, Effendi of Effesdar and Mustapha-Rasycheh, Effendi, Reys-ul-Kouttab, Ministers Plenipotentiary of His Highness the Grand Vizier.

The French Army in Egypt, anxious to give proof of its desire to halt the shedding of blood and to end the tragic quarrel between the French Republic and the Sublime Porte, agrees to evacuate Egypt as laid down in the present agreement, hoping that this concession may prove to be a path to the general pacification of Europe.

First Article

The French Army will retire with its arms, baggage and other possessions to Alexandria, Rosetta and Aboukir in order to embark and be taken to France

---

[77] With these words, he perhaps meant to draw attention to certain generals who, having come together in a private council, had decided to fight. An uprising at Alexandria designed to deliver the town over the English, the uncertainty of victory, the weariness and lack of enthusiasm of the troops as well as other considerations, just as worrying, all contributed to the wish to evacuate Egypt.

in its own ships, or such others as may be required supplied to them by the Sublime Porte; and in order that such ships may be made ready quickly it is agreed that one month after the ratification of this covenant the Sublime Porte will send a commissioner with fifty assistants to the castle at Alexandria.

Second Article

There will be a three month armistice in Egypt, counting from the date of signature of the present agreement; however, should the truce expire before the above mentioned ships provided by the Sublime Porte are ready, the said truce shall be extended until the embarkation shall be entirely completed. It is, of course, understood that all parties will do everything possible to ensure there is no disturbance of the calm between the Army and the population which is the object of the treaty.

Third Article

The transportation of the French Army will be governed by the regulations of the Commissioners appointed for this purpose by the Sublime Porte and by Commanding General Kléber. If, during the embarkation, there should be any disagreement between the Commissioners on this subject, a Commissioner will be nominated by Commodore Sidney Smith who will resolve the differences according to the Maritime Regulations of England.

Fourth Article

The positions at Katieh and Salheyeh will be evacuated by French troops on the eighth, or, at the latest, the tenth, day following the ratification of this convention. The town of Mansourah will be evacuated on the thirteenth day and Damiette and Belbeiss on the twentieth day. Suez will be evacuated six days before Cairo. Other positions on the east bank of the Nile will be evacuated on the tenth day; the delta will be evacuated fifteen days after Cairo. The west bank of the Nile and dependencies there will remain in French hands until Cairo is evacuated; however, in view of the fact that they must be occupied by French Army until all the troops have arrived from Upper Egypt, it may not be possible to evacuate the said west bank and dependencies until the expiration of the truce, if it is impossible to evacuate them earlier. The positions evacuated by the Army must be returned to the Sublime Porte in the state in which they were found.

Article Five

The town of Cairo will be evacuated on the fortieth day if possible or, at the latest, on the forty-fifth day, counting from the date of ratification of this treaty.

Article Six

It is expressly agreed that the Sublime Porte will take every care to ensure that the French troops occupying the various locations on the west bank of the Nile, as they return with their arms and equipment to their general headquarters, should not be harassed or molested on their way, either in their persons, their equipment or their honour, be it by the people of Egypt or by the troops of the Imperial Ottoman Army.

Article Seven
In accordance with the above article and to prevent any argument or antagonism, steps will be taken to ensure that Turkish troops are stationed at a sufficient distance from the French troops.

Article Eight
As soon as this present treaty is ratified, all Turkish soldiers and those of other nationalities who are subjects of the Sublime Porte, imprisoned or detained in France or by the French in Egypt, will be set at liberty and, reciprocally, all the French detained in the towns and seaports of the Ottoman empire, as well as those persons of whatever nationality attached to legations and consulates of France, will be set at liberty.

Article Nine
The restoration of their goods and property to the inhabitants and subjects on both sides, or the payment of equivalent value to them, will start immediately after the evacuation of Egypt, and will be regulated from Constantinople by the commissioners appointed for this duty.

Article Ten
No inhabitant of Egypt, of whatever religion, shall be threatened either as to his belongings or his person as a result of any dealings he may have had with the French during their occupation of Egypt.

Article Eleven
The French Army will receive from the Sublime Porte as well as from the courts of his allies, that is to say from Great Britain and Russia, such passports and safe conducts as are necessary to ensure its return to France.

Article Twelve
When the French Army has been embarked, the Sublime Porte and his allies promise that, until it arrives in France, it will not be harassed in any way. The Commanding General Kléber and the French Army in Egypt promise, for their part, to engage in no hostile action during this time, either against the ships or the countries of the Sublime Porte or his allies, and that the ships carrying the aforesaid army will not land on any coast other than that of France except under the most pressing necessity.

Article Thirteen
As a consequence of the above stipulated three month truce with the French Army to enable it to evacuate Egypt, the contracting parties agree that if, during the truce, without the knowledge of the allied captains, any French ships should arrive at Alexandria, they must leave immediately, having taken on water and essential stores. They will return to France furnished with passports from the allied courts; in the event that sundry of the above

mentioned ships should be in need of repair, they may remain until the repairs are carried out and leave immediately afterwards for France, like the others, by the first favourable wind.

Article Fourteen

The Commanding General Kléber may send a courier to France at once. The courier will be provided with the required safe-conducts so that he can advise the French Government of the evacuation of Egypt.

Article Fifteen

In acknowledgement of the fact that the French Army will require provisions for the three months during which it must evacuate Egypt, and for three further months from the day on which embarkation is complete, it is agreed that it will be provided with corn, meat, rice, barley and straw sufficient both for its stay and for the voyage, in accordance with the situation as now reported by the French plenipotentiaries. Such supplies as the Army is able to draw from its own stores after the ratification of the present convention are to be deducted from those that are to be provided by the Sublime Porte.

Article Sixteen

From the day of ratification of this convention, the French Army will not levy any taxes in Egypt; on the contrary, it must surrender to the Sublime Porte such normal taxes as might have been levied up to the time of the army's departure, as well as camels, dromedaries, ammunition, cannons and other items belonging to it which it does not intend to take with it, as well as the storehouses of grain accumulated from taxes already levied, and, finally, stores of food. These items will be inspected and valued by commissioners sent into Egypt by the Sublime Porte and by the Commander of the British forces, together with persons nominated by General Kléber, and received by the two former at the value set by them, up to the limit of three thousand bourses.[78] This sum will be required by the French Army to expedite transportation and embarkation. If the items listed above are not sufficient to produce this sum, the deficit will be advanced by the Sublime Porte, as a loan which will be reimbursed by the French Government, on the promissory notes of the commissioners nominated by General Kléber to receive the aforesaid money.

Article Seventeen

The French Army, having expenses to meet in order to carry out the evacuation of Egypt, will receive, after the ratification of this agreement, the sums shown below on the following dates:

On the 15th day ... 500 bourses
On the 30th day ... 500 bourses
On the 40th day ... 300 bourses

---

[78] A bourse was valued at about 1500 francs.

On the 50th day ... 300 bourses
On the 60th day ... 300 bourses
On the 70th day ... 300 bourses
On the 89th day ... 300 bourses

Finally, on the 90th day, 500 bourses, each of 500 Turkish piastres, which will be received on loan from the persons authorised by the Sublime Porte; in order to facilitate these instructions, the Sublime Porte will, immediately after the exchange of the ratifications, send his Commissioners into the town of Cairo and the other towns occupied by the army.

Article Eighteen
The taxes which the French may have collected after the date of ratification and before the notification of the present agreement to various parts of Egypt will be deducted from the total of 3000 bourses stipulated above.

Article Nineteen
To enable and expedite the evacuation of their positions, French transport vessels at present in Egyptian ports will, during the three months of the truce, be free to navigate from Damiette and Rosetta to Alexandria and from Alexandria to Rosetta and Damiette.

Article Twenty
The health of Europe demands the most rigorous precautions to ensure that the contagion of the plague should not be carried there. No person who is ill, or suspected of being infected by this disease shall be embarked. Sick persons afflicted with the plague or any other illness which prevents their trans-portation during the period of the embarkation, will remain in the hospitals where they happen to be under the protection of his highness the Supreme Vizier, and will be cared for by French medical officers, who will stay with them until such time as their health permits them to leave, which must take place as soon as possible. Articles 11 and 12 of this agreement will apply to them as to the rest of the army, and the Commander-in-Chief of the French Army undertakes to issue the strictest orders to the various officers com-manding the embarked troops that they must not be disembarked from the ships except at the ports designated by the medical officers, which offer the best facilities for the customary and essential quarantine.

Article Twenty-one
All the problems which may arise and which have not been foreseen by this agreement will be solved in a friendly fashion by the Commissioners appointed for this by his Highness the Supreme Vizier and by Commanding General Kléber, in such a way as to facilitate the evacuation.

Article Twenty-two
This covenant will only come into effect after the respective ratifications; these must be exchanged within eight days. Following the ratifications this covenant will be religiously observed by both parties.

Drawn up, signed and sealed with our respective seals at the conference camp at El Arich, on 4th Pluviôse of Year VIII of the Republic, 24th January 1800 (old style) and 28th of the moon of Chaaban, Year of the Hégire 1214.

Signed: *General of Division Desaix, Commandant Poussielgue, plenipotentiary of General Kléber, and their excellencies Mustapha-Rachid, Lord of Effesdar and Mustapha Rasycheh, Reys ul-Kouttab, plenipotentiaries of the Supreme Vizier.*

Certified copy of the French despatch handed to the Turkish Ministers in exchange for the authenticated Turkish copy.
Signed: *Desaix, Poussielgue.*

Ratification of the Commanding General of the French Army, placed at the end of the Turkish text, to remain in the possession of the Grand Vizier.
I, the undersigned, Commanding General of the French Army, approve and ratify the terms of the above treaty, having to implement in full the twenty-two articles contained therein, believing them to be an accurate representation of the French translation signed by the plenipotentiaries of the Grand Vizier and ratified by his Highness, a translation of which the meaning is always closely followed, except where, in view of some variation [in language], difficulties might result. At General Headquarters at Salheyeh, 8th Pluviôse, Year VIII [28th January 1800].
Kléber.

Certified Copy, General of Division, Chief of Staff.
Damas.

CHAPTER IX

MURAD BEY MAKES PEACE WITH THE FRENCH – ENGLISH OPPOSITION TO
TREATY – ULTIMATUM FAILS – THE BATTLE OF LACOUBÉ – THE SECOND
REVOLT IN CAIRO – ESBÉKIEH SQUARE – THE 'EXAMPLE' SET AT BULAQ –
SIEGE OF CAIRO – COLLECTION OF TAXES FROM INHABITANTS – ASSAS-
SINATION OF KLÉBER

As soon as the treaty was signed, Commodore Sidney Smith sent it to the
Court in England.

The publication of the agreement caused the most heartfelt joy in the
Army. To see again their household gods, their parents, their friends and
their lovers, what unanticipated happiness! What gratitude was due to a
general who had made every effort to achieve this! Yes, his name would
remain in our hearts as long as we should live. Nevertheless, as no joy is
unalloyed, our experience of it was diluted – or at least offset by a circumstance over which our General had no control. He was unable to pay us
more than one month's wages. How could we, with such a small sum,
manage to pay the debts we had contracted over eight months? How could
we maintain ourselves during the three months we must spend in Egypt
until embarkation? How to buy provisions for the voyage? Such is the
character of man; he worries continually over a future which may well not
occur in the manner he anticipates. We shall shortly see the truth of this
observation.

While waiting, the army withdrew to various locations in Egypt, having
given up to the Osmanlis[79] the fortifications previously occupied at the
various times fixed by the agreement at El Arich. How very punctual *we*
were in carrying out our promises! Our demi-brigade was sent to Cairo,
where it arrived on 28th Pluviôse, Year VIII [17th February 1800].

Murad Bey, against whom we had fought so long, doubtless fearing to
see his supreme authority in Egypt removed and of falling beneath the rule

---

[79] Turkish tribe, named after their founder, Osman.

of the Grand Sultan – of whom the Beys had, for a long while, made themselves independent – thought it to be in his own interest to transfer to our side, rather than to support the Turks. As a result he made his peace with us and, in the course of an interview with General Belliard, swore on his beard that the Grand Vizier would break his word, that for his part he would never again bear arms against us, and that for a long while he had borne arms only for his own defence. It must be said that this man during our stay in Egypt and Syria had shown nobility of spirit, and a courage to match the energy with which we pursued him, and that, in spite of reverses, he was always brave and patient. This character, so very much like that of the French, had earned our esteem and we sincerely hoped that he would take up the reins of government after our departure.

The result of our negotiations with the Grand Vizier could not be hidden from the Egyptians. To prevent the excesses which they might practise against us (for these people are like Italians – they give their support to those favoured by fortune), our General thought it wise to have the following proclamation published:

Kléber, Commanding General
To the Divan in Cairo and those of the various parts of Egypt

You have known for a long while of the fixed intention of the French Republic to maintain its age-old relations with the Ottoman Empire. My illustrious predecessor, General Bonaparte, frequently told you this. Since the fortunes of war brought us into this country, he neglected no effort to dispel the suspicions that had been aroused in the Supreme Porte, and which had involved him in an alliance as contrary to his own interests as to ours. The explanations he [Bonaparte] sent to the Court at Constantinople failed to re-establish the advantageous friendship between us. The advance of the Grand Vizier on Damascus provided him with more direct means of communication and he himself opened negotiations, which he then entrusted to me to bring to a conclusion, when important concerns compelled him to return to Europe. I have, today, concluded the negotiations, and place this land again in the hands of our ancient ally. The re-establishment of trade in Egypt will be the first result of this alliance. This treaty will be the beginning of a much needed peace among the nations of the West.

The principles by which we have governed Egypt are well known to you. We have upheld and respected your religion, your laws and customs and you have enjoyed the possession of all your property. We leave among you not one memory of violence; it is to you that the interests of the people of Egypt have been especially entrusted. You have been placed between them and the French, to ensure that there was no violation of the ancient customs of the country. These arrangements were made by the wisdom of my predecessor, and I have been conscious of the need to maintain them. The zeal with which you have carried out your honourable duties entitles you to the approbation

of all upright men and the special protection of the government which will replace you. The people of Egypt, guided by your council, will feel themselves to be placed under a well-established authority; the harmony which has always existed between them and you is both the result and the reward of your efforts. I hope that this unity will remain unaltered throughout the implementation of the treaty. If unexpected public disorder should occur, I shall be obliged to suppress it by force of arms.
Kléber.

That which our General had, like us, foreseen, and which he had wished to prevent, did not fail to occur. The barbarians with whom we had just been negotiating came out of their quarters, especially from Belbeiss, and, against the orders even of their own leaders, pushed forward and had the impudence to enter Cairo, where they swarmed on every corner and cross-roads, wandering here and there like bandits. They went so far as to entrench themselves in certain areas and, being well armed, on 12th Ventôse [3rd March 1800], they attacked all the French they could find. They cut many throats before their wicked plans could be understood. However, their lack of unity, and the shrewd action which was taken, made them pay dearly for the blood which they had spilled and they were driven from the town. Many of the bandits were captured and their chief [the Pasha] ordered that their heads should be cut off.

On the 19th Ventôse, Year VIII [10th March 1800], a letter from Smith indicated that the English Government was opposed to the implementation of the treaty signed by the Grand Vizier. This setback distressed the French Army as much as it overjoyed the Ladies of France, who made their joy manifest very loudly at the theatre that night. These 'mistresses of hearts' in Egypt where they had no fear of dangerous rivals, held, so to speak, the reins of government; our departure would tear them from their hands and put them back where they belonged.

It might be necessary here to explain the origin and reason for the title 'Ladies of France' in order to avoid any unfortunate interpretation. One day, wives of officers, soldiers and others arrived at the entrance to a restricted area. The sentry refused to let them through. This rudeness, as they called it, roused their ire and they complained bitterly about the lack of respect shown to them. 'How is it', they said, 'That the Ladies of France are not permitted to enter here?' 'Ah!', replied the sentry, presenting arms, 'Everything is permitted to the Ladies of France!'

The phrase was not forgotten. The sentry joked about it with his friends and shortly the whole army, learning of the incident, adopted the title. If the ladies who had followed us to Egypt did not equal Cleopatra in beauty, they did not fall short in coquetry. Certain that the French would never fall in love with the women of the country, for the reasons previously stated, these ladies affected an air of modesty which did not contrast badly with their habitual conduct, but greatly supported their act as helpless victims of love. On the altars on which he occasionally deposited his laurels, our ex-General did not sacrifice so lavishly to Mars that he forgot Venus. When the wife of one of the infantry captains captured his heart for a short time, her husband also benefited. Good things rained down upon him and he did not languish for long in the lower ranks. Meanwhile, in order to avoid his occasionally embarrassing presence, he was given an honourable mission to the French Government, and as the Captain travelled towards Toulon, Napoleon devoted the nights to consoling the lovely, lonely one.[80] This conquest, at least, did not cost him so dear as the siege of Acre. But let us return to more serious matters.

On 21st Ventôse [12th March 1800], all the troops were withdrawn from Cairo and took up positions nearby, while waiting for a clarification of the situation from the English Admiral. We soon found out that this was not in accordance with the wishes of the 'Ladies of France' from the following proclamation:

> Kléber, Commanding General, to the Army
>
> Soldiers,
> The command of the English fleet in the Mediterranean having passed into other hands, some delay in the implementation of the treaty which I concluded with the Grand Vizier has occurred: it should not last long. But, while we wait, we should remain on guard and retain that warlike attitude which inspires respect and fear when necessary. Soldiers, I am as responsible for your safety, as for your glory. I shall fulfil your expectations, but I demand of you your confidence and obedience in all circumstances.
> *Kléber.*

The Grand Vizier was again questioned, to try to discover what his position was; he swore that he did not share the intentions of the English Admiral [Keith][81]. Meanwhile, we refused to evacuate the Nile on the 23rd, as required by the treaty. We only changed position on the 25th, and placed ourselves in a state either to defend ourselves or to attack. The Grand Vizier urged us to cross the Nile, assuring us that he would keep his word. We avoided what we feared was a trap. We realised from the following letter that it was proposed to inflict humiliating terms upon us.

---

[80] The husband, Lieutenant Fourès, was captured by the British and, rather maliciously, returned to Alexandria, where he was angry to find his wife sharing the Commander-in-Chief's bed and board.
[81] Admiral George Keith Elphinstone (see Short Biographies).

From headquarters, Cairo, 27th Ventôse, Year VIII [18th March 1800]
Commanding General Kléber, to the Army

The following is a letter which has been sent to me by the Commander of the English fleet of the Mediterranean.

From His Majesty's ship, *Queen Charlotte*, 8th January 1800[82]

Sir,

I have to inform you that I have received definite orders from His Majesty not to consent to any capitulation from the French Army which you command in Egypt and Syria, at least unless it lays down its arms and accepts prisoner of war status, and surrenders all the ships and munitions in the port and town of Alexandria to the allied powers. In the event of capitulation, I should not be able to permit any troops to return to France unless exchanged. I feel, also, that I should inform you that all vessels with French troops on board sailing from this country with passports supplied by others than those with the right to issue them will be forced by the captains of the ships under my command to return to Alexandria; finally, ships which are found returning to Europe with passports provided as a result of a separate capitulation with the allied powers will be held as a prize and all those on board considered to be prisoners of war.
Signed: *Keith.*

Soldiers, we shall know how to answer such insolence with victories.
Prepare yourselves for battle.
Kléber.

What thoughts resulted from reading this order from the Court in London! What lack of respect for the other powers, its allies! Men given passports by these courts to be held as prisoners of war! This would imply that they had no right to issue them. It is worthy of remark that, throughout a revolution the seeds of which had come from England, the government of that island had never fought us except by means of other peoples (if one excepts the war at sea). These they placed in front of them to ward off our blows, and then profited from the blood spilled by those who had helped and shielded them. It appeared, as well, that their agents or informants had only told them of our dreadful situation and of our small numbers in Egypt, and had concealed the courage and noble pride of this little army, so that it was believed that we were already beaten and nothing remained but to lead us away in chains. This government imagined that it held us already within the narrow circle of Popilius. The only reply worthy of us was that given by our General. He well knew our sentiments.

---

[82] The date of the letter implied that the Convention of El Arich had been disavowed before it was even signed. The British were acting on reports from September 1799 that the Army of Egypt was on the verge of collapse.

This change of intention by the English cabinet made necessary a similar change in the policy of the Porte, so that General Kléber, having received no reply to his ultimatum within the time fixed, caused his troops to march on Lacoubé, two miles from Cairo, which they reached on the 29th Ventôse [20th March] at dawn.

The troops were formed up in battalion squares, with a cannon at each corner; most of the artillery were drawn up and protected by several battalions. On the other side were the cavalry with the Commanding General at their head. This disposition gave the appearance of a formidable army, which might have been taken for a hundred thousand men, whereas it was, in reality, only ten thousand.

It was in this formation that we marched towards the enemy until we were within cannon range. When we got there our artillery fired with such precision that the enemy's advance guard was compelled to give ground and retire quickly to their base camp at Matarieh. We pursued them closely and attacked the camp itself, invading it despite the most stubborn opposition, and taking possession of everything in it: baggage and fourteen cannon fell into our hands, and the ground was covered with corpses.

The engagement was so hot that the leaders of the enemy did not even have time to gather and carry off their pipes (items that they thought as necessary and as precious as their swords). It was vital not to give the enemy time to catch their breath or to regroup; therefore we pursued them, and, the better to do this, we left everything in the village of Matarieh: cannons, baggage and even, they say, six hundred Osmanlis who had escaped the massacre.

Murad Bey, who by chance was with the Grand Vizier, to whom he had gone with the approval of Kléber during the truce, sent a negotiator to ask for peace. The French General sent a message back to tell him to keep away from the guns, which he did, and appeared no more during the fight, save at a distance. The Vizier also wished to negotiate, but received the following reply. 'Let those who got you into this mess come today to rescue you from it, the ones who remained prudently in their ships at a reasonable distance from danger.' So, it was in vain that they asked for a cease-fire.

It was equally useless for them to call upon their Prophet Mohammed, or to rely on help from the two hundred men who were supposed to come and destroy us, in accordance with a divine revelation which was said to have been received. They were, instead, compelled to continue to beat a retreat and we pursued them vigorously. On the first day we chased them to Alouka, six miles from Cairo, and cleared them out of the place so quickly that they again abandoned an immense amount of baggage and camp equipment.

The gunfire which we heard all night warned the General that there was a disturbance in Cairo, so he decided to send troops there: these consisted of a battalion of my regiment, including myself, and two from the 25th, one of the 61st and four cannon, commanded by General Lagrange.[83] We marched off an hour after midnight on the 30th Ventôse [20th March 1800].

We had scarcely reached Lacoubé when we saw an immense body of cavalry coming towards us. Instead of distracting ourselves by fighting we carefully avoided them and continued on our way to Cairo. Nevertheless, they harassed us and from time to time we had to hold them off with volleys of gunfire. This difficulty did not prevent us from reaching headquarters at three in the afternoon. There we found that numbers of Mameluks and Osmanlis had penetrated the town and provoked an uprising amongst the people; they had made various attempts to capture the headquarters and sundry French positions. They had the more hope of success as we had only left our sick and wounded there – in other words, all those who had not been able to follow us onto the plains against the enemy army.

On the first day of Germinal, Year VIII [21st March 1800], the battalion to which I was attached was posted to Esbékieh, where, in the morning, everything was peaceful, but at eight o'clock, when we tried to communicate with the inhabitants of the French quarter in order to bring help to endangered Europeans, we were met by the most stubborn and well-organised resistance. Several roads were blocked by impassable barricades. Those exposed in the lead were overrun, their commanding officer, several other officers and soldiers having been dangerously wounded. The rebels, emboldened by this retreat, started to attack us, swooping on us with the speed of an eagle. The boldest of them, as was their custom, came and planted little flags in front of us and well onto the main square, while a crowd of others, no less daring, went from house to house, knocking down the dividing walls and obtaining access to the houses which our troops were defending. These were forced to give ground and lost several men. When the rest of them tried to imitate their flag-bearers and come close to us, they certainly found out that we were not firing in the air. Volleys of musket and artillery fire, repeated several times and very accurate, tore holes in their ranks and, after the most unbelievable efforts, those of them who had not already bitten the dust were persuaded that they would do better not to attack our front. They then decided to advance on our flanks by way of the Reynier house and through the Copt quarter. By this means they would have been able to attack our Headquarters; to prevent this, we fired left and right, which soon halted them and did much to moderate their ardour.

On the following day they again attacked us in the same way, but with less success than previously. We were not a little surprised to see them return on the third day with cannon. These were the guns we had captured

---

[83] Joseph Lagrange (1763–1836), Count from 1810.

and foolishly left at Matarieh, without even spiking them. This lack of foresight would have been fatal for us except for the arrival of the General with the whole army. The army had pushed the Grand Vizier back into the desert; the Arabs had pillaged the enemy baggage while we had captured several field guns and a considerable amount of camp equipment. Before this last victory part of the army, consisting largely of the cavalry and the general staff, had found itself exposed to great danger at Koraïm, sixty miles from Cairo; our General himself nearly lost his life there. He was, at one time, surrounded by Mameluks, who were cautious about approaching him. His skill with the sabre protected him until the dragoons arrived to extricate him.

When our army arrived, it made ready on both flanks either to attack or to defend itself. The insurgents retreated into the houses and dug deep ditches across the roads, setting up impenetrable barricades, while we fortified the Headquarters with redoubts, connecting trenches and earthworks. The main body of the army sealed the town tightly, and it was as difficult for them to get in as for the enemy to get out, but the army had the advantage of being able to bombard the town, which it did from time to time. Alarmed at their position and restricted in their movements, the Mameluks and Osmanlis asked for negotiations to be held, and this was agreed to.

The discussions took place on the 10th Germinal [30th March 1800] in a tent set up on the Square, mid-way between the opposing forces. The representatives of the Mameluks and the people of Cairo on the one hand, and General Dumas,[84] on behalf of the Commander-in-Chief, on the other concluded a treaty whereby the enemy agreed to evacuate the Square within forty-eight hours, handing over to us their gun-emplacements and main positions the next day to ensure they kept their word.

When an attempt was made on the following day to take possession of these posts, those who defended them asked for a delay of some hours, saying that they had received no orders from their leaders; the leaders blamed this on the stubborn disobedience of their soldiers. This manoeuvre made it plain that they sought only to gain time in which to fortify their positions. So, in order not to fall victim to their ruse or their treachery, we reopened hostilities on the 12th. On the 13th, at eleven o'clock in the evening, the area behind the Copt quarter was attacked. The enemy fire was

---

[84] Thomas Alexandre Dumas, also known as Davy de La Pailleterie (1762–1806) (natural son of Alexandre Davy, marquis de La Pailleterie, and one Marie Dumas). Father of the author Alexandre Dumas (1803–1870) and grandfather of Alexandre Dumas *fils* (1824–1895).

deadly; our column was compelled to retreat, but soon after, with redoubled bravery, it carried terror and death into the ranks of the enemy and regained the ground. It would have gained more had not a superior order arrived, halting its advance. Between triumph and disaster there is often only a step; our column was attacked the next day by stronger forces and compelled to give up part of its conquest. Many of our soldiers perished there, and many of our grenadiers were made prisoner but were later returned (which is not usual amongst barbaric people).

Murad Bey, who, as already mentioned above, had asked for peace, achieved the object of his plan and, as reward, obtained the governorship of a province. Wishing to strengthen his possessions he sent emissaries to the Mameluks of Ibrahim Bey to bring them onto his side. He would certainly have won them all over, but for the opposition of the Osmanlis, who had learned of these plots; if they had been entirely successful they would have been of help to us. There had been dissension between these two leaders since the Grand Vizier had made known his friendship for Ibrahim and his contempt for Murad. He had promised important positions to the first and nothing to the second. This rivalry would have been useful to us in the re-conquest of Cairo.

It was under these circumstances that Rosetta [sic], Imperial Commissioner and famous schemer, thought to win the trust of the French, in order to betray them more completely; in pursuit of this aim he pretended to negotiate on behalf of Bulaq, which was also in revolt. Thus, he made us believe that the majority of the inhabitants of that town were holding out the hand of friendship to us. By this means we were persuaded that a proclamation, containing promise of an amnesty, would convert all the rest. So, one of these lines was issued, and the battalion, of which I was a member, was despatched to take it to Bulaq.

We set off, the band playing before us and olive branch in hand, as when we entered a French town in triumph. Imagine our indignation when, as we entered the town, we were met with brutal volleys of cannon fire! We saw clearly that it would take more than the sound of music to make them listen. So we terminated our triumphal march. General Dumas arrived and spoke to the people, who answered that they would do as was being done in the capital. On hearing this, we returned to Cairo to share the work and the fate of the Army. Hostilities continued and attacks were renewed on both sides. Sometimes the town was bombarded, sometimes a few houses were seized and immediately burned. The enemy did the same to the Copt quarter (the only one we occupied) whenever they were able to.

On the 25th Germinal of Year VIII [14th April 1800], the insolent and miserable town of Bulaq was attacked vigorously at several points. It was defended stubbornly at first, but after several hours of fighting the gates were broken down and the town entered in strength. How dearly this unfortunate town paid for its foolish rebellion! I saw most of its inhabitants bayoneted there, a huge number of houses burned and everything pillaged. After this sad and terrible punishment, no one who had seen Bulaq before would have recognised it now. Such are the results of the awful power of war.

On the 28th in the evening, a mine blew up the Reynier house, which was, for the enemy, an unassailable refuge. Many rebels were buried beneath the ruins, some crushed under the rubble, others incinerated in the fires which leaped from the debris. An unbearable smell was spewed from the flames. Finally attacks were launched on all sides; all the cannon in the fortresses were brought into action, and bombs were fired over the town and crashed onto the buildings. Several positions were seized and set on fire. It was a terrible sight! It was as if hell itself had been carried into the centre of the town. Those who had brought these horrors on themselves were terrified and begged to capitulate. For answer they received the terrible words, 'No quarter'. After having been refused several times, they were at last listened to. We had lost very many men, but the enemy losses were infinitely greater.

During the course of this unforgettable siege (it had lasted for over a month), the losses of the Mameluks and Osmanlis, in men as well as in munitions, the scarcity and high price of food, the internal dissension, the discontent of the people, all forced the enemy to accept the terms which we proposed and we ended the operation by the reading of the following proclamation:

From the Headquarters at Cairo, 2nd Floréal, Year VIII [22nd April 1800]
Kléber, Commanding General, to the Army

Soldiers,
To spare you loss of blood, I have hurried on negotiations and military operations. The greatest obstacle I have encountered is the difficulty of reassuring the natives of the country as to their safety from pillage and devastation. The example of Bulaq, where I permitted you, for an instant, to satisfy your legitimate desire for vengeance, is terrible in their eyes. I have contrived to calm them; I have promised them safety and protection, both for their persons and their goods; they have immediately ceased to make difficulties about the withdrawal of Ottoman troops.

Soldiers, when your commanding officer makes promises in the name of the army, it is for you to fulfil them. I rely in this matter equally on your obedience and your understanding of what is in your own interest. One single excess could render illusory the surrender which has just been concluded. Therefore, do not merely be content with refraining from the least disorder yourselves, but also ensure that none is committed by any mob of

men who, hidden while dangers surrounded you, come forth only when the peril is past in order to crown their dishonour. I forbid, therefore, all pillage, and refer back to my order of the 27th Germinal on the same subject.[85]
Kléber.

On the same day, we took control of part of the town and, above all, of the batteries. On the 5th, the enemy evacuated it entirely and was escorted as far as the forward positions by the first division. Our army then proceeded to camp near Bulaq, having marched in triumph through several roads and areas of Cairo. The pressing needs of the army made it vital to impose heavy taxes on the townspeople, which annoyed them greatly, so that many of them abandoned their homes, or pretended to.

Generally speaking these people are so in love with their money that they would rather cut their throats than part with a penny of it. On the 13th Floréal [3rd May 1800] it was again necessary to blockade the town in order to stop these desertions. On the 15th [5th May 1800], when the first division came back, the army entered the town and garrisoned it and began to gather in the taxes. The people, in order to arouse the Commanding General's pity, instead of bringing money, brought dishes, silver knives and forks and jewellery. But, as their motives were understood, all these things were accepted and promptly sold to the Jews and Copts who made an immense profit. Of the ten months of taxes due to the army, two were paid, and it was said that four more were obtained from merchandise confiscated when the town was captured.

There was then a rumour that Kléber was about to leave on a visit to the delta and the sea coast. The rumour started up gossip. 'What's happened to the money which was gathered in taxes? There would have been more than enough there to give us our back-pay. What's the idea behind going off to visit the coast, he who, throughout the siege, never set foot outside his office? He's going to act like Bonaparte', people said, 'He's off to the safety of France, taking with him the immense wealth obtained at the cost of our toil and sweat!' Does this not show the character of the common people and the soldier? If they are discontented they imagine follies, and attribute to innocent actions the most ridiculous, false motives. They were today censuring a General whose loss would soon occasion them the most bitter regret and many tears.

Learning of the rumours and damaging stories that were going around, Kléber, to check them, decided to alter his travel plans. On the 14th Prairial [3rd June 1800], the appearance of several enemy sails off the coast was announced, and as a result we were ordered to leave at once. The

---

[85] This Order of the Day imposed the death penalty on pillagers.

Commanding General soon accompanied us. Everyone put their own construction on this: one believed that we were threatened with a new raid, others said that this rumour was spread around in order to disguise the departure, or flight, of Kléber. On the 19th we arrived at El Rahmanieh, where we found many troops already there. The General, able to verify with his own eyes the presence of an enemy fleet and, knowing nothing of its intentions, thought it proper to leave us there in reserve and he himself, unfortunately, returned to Cairo.

As he had ordered, we established ourselves at Salmieh, a small village at the south of the delta on the right bank of Rosetta. But what was our misery, I could almost say our despair, when we were informed, shortly afterwards, that Kléber was dead, that he had been cravenly assassinated! No, we could not have wept more bitterly for a beloved father, than we wept for our leader, the friend of the soldier. Where could a worthy successor be found for him, one who would have for us the same affection as this generous hero? Where to find him? The answer to this question was given in the following proclamation:

From General Headquarters in Cairo, 26th Prairial, Year VIII [15th June 1800]
Abdallah Menou, General of Division, Acting Commander-in-Chief of the army. To the army:

Soldiers,
A dreadful assault has taken from us a general who you loved and respected. An enemy, deserving only of the hatred and rage of the entire world, an enemy unable to overcome the French commanded by the brave Kléber, has, like the coward he is, sent in his place an assassin. I denounce to you, I denounce to the world, the name of the Grand Vizier, leader of the army which you destroyed on the plains of Matarieh and Heliopolis. He it is, who, together with the Aga of his Janissaries, placed the dagger in the hand of one named Soleyman El-Halebi, who left Gaza thirty-two days ago. It is he who has, by the blackest of murders, deprived us of a leader whose memory must be dear to every good Frenchman.

Soldiers, at your head, Kléber had scattered this mob of barbarians who swept down upon Egypt from Europe and Asia. Kléber, directing your invincible cohorts, re-conquered the whole of Egypt in ten days. Kléber, had so restored the finances of the Army that all arrears have been paid and pay is now up to date. Kléber, by his wise administration, had reformed most of the abuses which are almost inseparable from large undertakings.

The greatest tribute you can pay to the memory of Kléber, is to maintain that proud and imposing demeanour which has caused your enemies to tremble wherever you have travelled. It is up to you to subject yourselves to that discipline which is the strength of an army. It is up to you to remind yourselves continually that you are Republicans, that everywhere you must set an example of morality and obedience to your leaders, just as you set an example of courage and audacity in battle.

Soldiers, my seniority of rank has brought me, provisionally, to the command of the Army. I can offer you nothing but an unbounded loyalty to the Republic, to liberty and to the prosperity of France. I invoke the shades of Kléber, I invoke the genius of Bonaparte, and, marching together with you, we shall work for the well-being of the Republic.

The army will shortly be informed of all the details of this dreadful assassination, as well as of the actions which will be taken to find and punish the killers and their accomplices.
Abd. Menou

The most persuasive eloquence could not solace the army for a loss which it felt to be irreparable. The army experienced such sincere regret for the man they felt to have been father-like, that the soldiers were able to think of nothing but his memory. Quite convinced that this great general had been concerned solely with the well-being of his soldiers and their safe return to France, they now felt the full extent of the loss they had suffered. The above announcement, though wisely and elegantly expressed, far from relieving the general despondency, only deepened it.

The first name [Abdallah] of the new general was no help to him: the republicanism of the army had not stifled the regard for convention and the religious ideas which we had all acquired from our early education, and the customs of our country. He was a renegade, they said, a man who had renounced his country in order to embrace the law of Mohammed and to place a turban on his own head; is he then fit to command us? He has bound his fate and his affections to a woman of this country. Will he, then, contemplate abandoning his new family and returning to France where he would be despised? Far from negotiating with our enemies, far from carrying out the wishes of Kléber, will he not do everything he can to keep us in Egypt as supporters of his power and to be his companions in his voluntary exile? Such were the subjects of conversation, which, if they were not free of prejudice, yet appeared to have some truth in them. But let us pay the last honours to him whom we mourned.

CHAPTER X

GENERAL KLÉBER'S FUNERAL – THE ADMINISTRATION OF GENERAL
MENOU – IN PRAISE OF MENOU – NEWS OF MARENGO

From the moment of Kléber's death, the mournful sounds of artillery
salutes could be heard every half-hour. On the day of the funeral, 28th
Prairial [17th June], from early in the morning, these salvoes, coming from
the citadel, repeated by all the forts and echoing around, announced that
the army was about to render the last honours to him. The cortège, leaving
Headquarters in Esbékieh Square, to the sound of five cannon shots and a
general volley of musketry fire, traversed the entire town, proceeding to lay
the mortal remains of the General in the camp which had been fortified on
Ibrahim Bey's farm. The following was the order of march: a detachment of
cavalry as an advance guard, five field-pieces, the 22nd Light Infantry, the
1st Cavalry Regiment, the Guides, dismounted, and the band of the entire
garrison, playing music suitable to the tragic occasion.

The body of the General, enclosed in a lead coffin, was carried on an
elegant funeral carriage, spread with black velvet sprinkled with silver
drops, and surrounded with trophies. The sword of the hero was placed on
the coffin and the carriage was drawn slowly along by six horses draped in
black and bearing white plumes.

General Menou was preceded by the crêpe-decked colours of the Corps
of Guides, and escorted by generals, the Headquarters staff and then
Kléber's aides-de-camp. Next came the general commanding the camp,
together with his staff officer, the engineering corps, the members of the
Institute, the commissariat, the medical officers, administrators, the
mounted guides, Hussein Kachef, commissioner of Murad Bey accompanied by his Mameluks, the Agas, the Cadis,[86] the Sheikhs, the Ulémas,

---

[86] A Muslim judge.

the Greek bishops, monks and priests, the Copts, the Catholics, various governing bodies of the town, the 9th and the 13th Demi-Brigades, the Navy, the Sappers, the Greek Battalion, the Copt Militia, the Dromedary Regiment, the Foot Artillery, the Cavalry Corps, the mounted Mameluks and the Syrians.

A detachment of French cavalry brought up the rear. At eleven o'clock the cortège arrived on the parade ground of the Institute, where the troops formed into a circle. The sound of musketry and the five cannon announced the resting place of our General, now placed briefly upon a dais surrounded by lighted sconces.

The Headquarters staff dismounted to pay their respects to the remains of their Commander, and soldiers of every rank and of every part of the army pressed forward spontaneously to cast wreaths of laurel and cypress on the tomb, while paying their tribute with words of the deepest and most sincere sorrow.

M. Fourrier, the French Commissioner to the Divan, charged by General Menou to express the universal sorrow, now took up his position, near to the Staff Major and senior civil and military officers, on a bastion looking down on the army, which was drawn up in battle order. In an emotional voice he spoke the following words:

Frenchmen,
Amidst this funeral pomp, which is a tribute, fleeting but sincere, to the general sorrow, I am about to recall a name dear to you, which has already achieved an honoured place in history. Three days have passed since Kléber, Commanding General of the French Army of the East, was taken from you. This man, so often spared by death in battle, whose military deeds have resounded on the banks of the river Rhine, of the Jordan and the Nile, has now perished, helpless, under the blows of an assassin.

When, in future, you gaze on this place where all around has been devoured by flames and stand in the midst of ruins, a testament for years to come to the ravages of a terrible but necessary war, you will see this lonely house, where a hundred Frenchmen held out for two whole days against a capital in revolt, and the combined efforts of the Mameluks and Ottomans. Your eyes will rest, involuntarily, on this fatal spot where the dagger cut short the days of the victor of Maastricht and Heliopolis; you will say, 'It is there that our leader and friend died. His voice, brutally silenced, could not call us to his aid'. Oh, how many arms would have been raised in his defence! How many of you would have longed for the honour of casting yourselves between him and the assassin! I call you to witness, brave cavalry, who sped to save him on the heights of Koraïm and, in a moment, scattered the surrounding enemy throng. This life, which he owed to your courage, he lost through that over-confidence which led him to stroll, unarmed, apart from those who would have guarded him.

When he had driven the troops of Youssef Pasha, Grand Vizier of the Ottoman Empire, from Egypt, he cut down or put to flight the seditious, the traitors and the ungrateful. Then, loathing the cruelty which marked Oriental victories, he swore that he would bring honour to the name of France by his clemency, as he had made it glorious by feats of arms. He kept this promise faithfully. He found no one guilty, none of them died; only the victor perished amongst his trophies. Not the loyalty of his guards, not his noble and soldierly appearance, nor even the zeal of so many of the soldiers who loved him, could protect him from this dreadful death. Thus ends so fine, so honourable a career! It is here that so much toil, danger and such dazzling service is brought to a close!

One man, filled with the dark rage of fanaticism, is appointed, by the leaders of a beaten army in Syria, to assassinate the French general. He hurries across the desert, stalks his victim for a month, the deadly opportunity occurs and the crime is committed. Faithless negotiators, cowardly generals, this is your crime; it will be as infamous as your defeat. The French yielded their positions to you under the assurance of a treaty; you were at the gates of the capital, while the English refused to open the seaports. So you demanded that the French should abide by a treaty which your allies had broken. You offered only the desert as a refuge. Their hearts all blazed with indignation, insulted honour and consciousness of danger: within three days your armies were scattered and destroyed. You lost three encampments and more than sixty field pieces, you were driven from all the towns and forts between Damiette and Säid. Only the consideration of the French General prolonged the siege of Cairo, that wretched town where you spilled the blood of unarmed men. You watched as that multitude of soldiers, gathered from the depths of Asia, were scattered and died in the desert: then you entrusted their vengeance to an assassin.

But, citizens, what benefit do our enemies expect to obtain from this hideous crime? By striking down this victorious General, do they hope that the soldiers under his command will disappear? And if a so base a hand can cause so many tears to be spilled, can it also prevent the French Army from being led by a commander worthy of it? Certainly not. And if, now, extraordinary abilities are required; if, to bear the burden of this momentous enterprise, some individual of nobler spirit than ever before known is needed, one possessing a boundless devotion to the glory of the nation, citizens, you will find these qualities united in his successor. He was valued by Bonaparte and by Kléber, and today takes their place. Thus there will be no delay in the achievement of the honourable hopes of the French, nor in the despair of their enemies.

Soldiers of the Army, who unite the names of Italy, the Rhine and Egypt, you find yourselves placed by fate in extraordinary circumstances. The eyes of the world are upon you; even more important, your sublime courage is the admiration of your native land. Its gratitude consecrates your victories. Never forget that you are here under the watchful eyes of that great man who has been chosen by the fortune of France to establish the destiny of a state weakened by public discord. His genius is by no means curbed by the seas which separate us from our fatherland. He lives among you now, he drives you on, excites you to courage, gives you confidence in your leaders, without which your bravery is useless; he inspires in you all the military virtues of which he has left you so many, and such glorious, examples. May the blessings of a stable government crown the efforts of the French!

It is thus, worthy warriors, that you will enjoy the honours due to true citizens. You will talk among yourselves of this far country which you have twice conquered; the innumerable armies you have crushed, be it through the far-sighted audacity of Bonaparte which sought them in Syria, or when the invincible courage of Kléber scattered them in the very heart of Egypt. What wonderful memories you will carry back to the bosom of your families! May they bring happiness that sweetens the bitterness of your regrets. You will often pronounce the beloved name of Kléber as you reminisce, and never without emotion; you will say 'he was a friend to soldiers, he saved them bloodshed and lessened their sufferings.'

It is true that the troubles of the army were his daily concern and he thought of nothing but how to ease them. How terribly he was distressed by the delay, then inevitable, in paying the Army, despite the special taxes which were the object of the only harsh orders he ever gave. He devoted himself to regulating the finances of the army, and you well know how successful he was. He placed the control of it in the hands of honest men, chosen from those who enjoyed public respect. He was contemplating setting up an organisation which would comprise all parties in the government. Death brutally interrupted this worthy project.

He leaves a memory dear to all men of goodwill; no one wished more, or deserved better, to be loved. He grew ever more attached to his old friends, for they possessed qualities of character similar to his own. Their justifiable sorrow will, at least, find some consolation in the knowledge of the army's esteem and the universality of its mourning.

Unite in your homage, Frenchmen, for you are but a single warrior family, called by your country to her defence, and which a common fate has brought together on this foreign soil. Your homage this day will include, too, those heroes who, on the battlefields of Syria, Aboukir and Heliopolis, turned their dying eyes and their last thoughts towards France.

O, Caffarelli,[87] model of unselfishness and virtue, so considerate of others, so stoical in yourself, you also must be honoured at these obsequies, for you were united in close friendship with Kléber.

---

[87] General Caffarelli died following the Siege of Acre where his elbow was smashed by a cannon ball: he did not survive the resulting amputation.

And you, Kléber, of glorious memory, ill-fated, in that this ceremony is followed by no other, rest in peace, kindly and beloved shade, among the monuments of glory and the arts. Rest in earth so long renowned. May your name be linked with that of Germanicus, Titus and Pompey and so many great leaders and scholars who have left, like you, immortal memories in this land.

A reverential silence followed for a moment the torrent of tears which the orator's words had called forth. The troops then marched off by platoons, halting in front of the sarcophagus, and firing a third volley of musketry, while artillery, out in the country, in the citadel, the forts and entrenched positions, made the neighbourhood of Bulaq resound.[88]

Who would believe that, in spite of all the proof of Kléber's death, there were still some minds so bizarre or wicked as to claim that all these ceremonies were nothing but a trick, that the General had left for France in accordance with his original intentions and that his empty coffin had been borne with pomp to the grave only as a cover for his flight. But the visible signs of his demise, and the punishment of his assassin and their accomplices quickly put a stop to such absurd ideas.

As a matter of fact the assassin admitted his crime and appeared to glory in it, but he did not enjoy his glory long, for he was condemned to having his hand cut off and to be impaled, this being the custom of the country. Three members of the Divan in Cairo were beheaded for having failed to reveal Soleyman's intention, of which they had known and of which they were found guilty.

So now we come to the administration of General Menou. A better idea of it will be given by quoting official papers than from our own knowledge. The following piece will serve to give the reader an insight into the views of our new commander.

---

[88] 'Kléber's remains were transported to the Chateau d'If. In 1814 the King ordered them to be transferred to Marseilles to receive the last honours and to be placed in a worthy tomb. This year [1818], at the request of Lieutenant General Dumas, once Kléber's Staff Officer, and on the advice of the Ministry of War, His Majesty decided that the body should be transferred to Strasbourg, the town where Kléber was born, there to be buried with the honour appropriate to such a great leader, to his noble character and the services he rendered to the state.' (*Journal de Paris*, Jeudi, 16 Juilliet, 1818.)

Cairo Headquarters, 3rd Messidor, Year VIII [22nd June 1800]
From J. Menou, Commander-in-Chief, to the General of *Division Verdier*[89]

I have no ambition, Citizen General, other than to be worthy of the esteem and trust of the troops, while serving the Republic with all the fervour of which I am capable. Each day, every minute will be devoted to the well-being of the Army, and I shall count as wasted every moment which I do not employ in its interest.

The barbarous Osmanlis, who, unlike the French, are without courage, use instead the coward's weapons, the dagger and poison. Faithless and without law, they have, as you know, held captive, contrary to human rights, the negotiator, *Chef de Brigade* Baudot. I have here a hundred and fifty prisoners of war who will be answerable for his safety. I have informed Jaffa of this, and I have also told the English, who are, perhaps, no more scrupulous than their allies.

As for our situation in Egypt, it is for the government of the Republic to give us our orders. Egypt is now such a weighty factor in the European balance of power that only our Government can assess the effects of our actions. I trust that we shall soon hear from them.

Vigilance and action are needed, Citizen General, regular communication both with me, and with the provinces in your neighbourhood, must be carefully maintained and all will be well.

I shall always ensure, by means of daily orders, that the Army is given all necessary information and, finally, I shall supply newspapers. Be good enough, Citizen General, to cause this letter to be read out to all the troops under your command.

This letter appeared to have been written in order to prepare us to resign ourselves. Everyone knew enough about General Menou's inclinations to feel no astonishment at his words; a supporter of the colony in Egypt, he counted on the expected orders from the French Government to prolong his stay – and ours – in this foreign land. He showed his intentions even more clearly in the following communication.

From Cairo Headquarters, 8th Messidor, Year VIII [27th June 1800]
From Commanding General Menou to the French Oriental Army

Generals, officers, non-commissioned officers and men,
You should be made aware of the whole facts. Here they are:

The French Government, having learned in Year VI that the enemies of the Republic were making plans to seize Malta and Egypt, resolved to thwart them. Trade in the Levant, which raised nearly fifty million francs annually, made their actions essential. The expedition to Malta and Egypt was ordered.

---

[89] Named after its General, Jean Antoine Verdier (1767–1839), Count from 1808.

Bonaparte was placed in command. He had arranged for a French ambassador to arrive in Constantinople at the same time that the Army set sail. In fact the Sultan was never informed of the government's views.[90] Our enemies, the English and the Russians, were quick to take advantage of this fact and forced the Sultan to join the coalition which has for many years fought against our Revolution and our liberty.

Turkish armies, under English control, were disembarked at Aboukir and at Damiette; you drove them back into the sea. Another army, commanded by the Grand Vizier in person, marched on Syria. Negotiations took place. A surrender, on which I will make no comment, was concluded. You are aware with what treachery it was breached; you will remember with what indignation you learned that it was intended to make you prisoners of war as if you had lost two or three battles, yet you had triumphed everywhere! The Ottoman Army advanced; you attacked it at Matarieh and at Heliopolis, in a moment it was scattered. Some remnants of this horde threw themselves upon Cairo and you were compelled to besiege the town which surrendered after a month of blockade. You well know of the brutal attack by means of which a commander whose memory we all revere was taken from you. You could not be conquered on the field of battle; our enemies have had to resort to a dagger, thinking by these foul means to demoralise the French Army. They little thought that the murder of Kléber served only to redouble your courage and vigilance. Let all the East gather against you, you will avenge the life of your General in their blood.

But who, henceforth, will lead you? Those who, alone, have that right; the Government of the French Republic. They alone have the authority to ratify or reject whatever terms have been agreed, to decide what should be the future nature of the relationship between the French Army and the enemy powers. All those (and I am confident of everyone), all those, I repeat, who wish to hear only the voice of honour, of love of the Republic and the national interest, will feel that by the path of honour and legality alone can a treaty with our enemies be concluded. Were I to follow my own wishes, were I to forget for one moment that I am a Republican, could I place my own happiness above the public good, like you I should not hesitate for a moment to wish to return to our own country.

But no, my good Republicans, neither you nor I think like that. We are guided only by the best interest of the Republic. If it is necessary we shall fight and we shall win. If we are to negotiate, we shall listen to the proposals put to us, but no treaty can be implemented that is not ratified by the Government. You all know Bonaparte, who led you so often to victory. It is he, in his position as First Consul, who will direct us and make plain our progress; he will be aware of everything and from the centre will inform us of the national will.

---

[90] Talleyrand was supposed to go to Constantinople to arrange a treaty with the Turks. He did not in fact do so, having no interest in furthering Napoleon's career.

I have spoken the truth to you, I shall never do anything else; following the examples of Bonaparte and Kléber, I shall strive to earn your confidence and respect. I shall never forget your interests nor cease to seek your well-being. Kléber had begun to re-establish the finances of the army; I shall complete his work.

Henceforth your pay will always be assured, outstanding debts will be paid; I shall endeavour to eliminate all abuses. But remember, it takes a long while to correct a wrong which took only a moment to commit. Obedience to officers of all ranks, strict discipline and morality is what I ask of the army; it is what I have the right to demand and I shall continue to remind you of it. But we are Republicans and shall behave fittingly. When, one day, we are back in our own country, we shall all be proud that we were part of an expedition which, today, has become of such importance in the balance of power in the universe.
Abd. J. Menou.

No matter how unpleasant it was to contemplate an indefinite stay in Egypt, to give up, perhaps forever, all hope of our native land, the knowledge that it was in the interest of the French Government, either to maintain its [Egyptian] conquest, or to withdraw intact an army which might well be useful elsewhere, did much to sweeten the bitterness of our feelings, and stiffen our resolve to play our part. 'If they wish to establish and maintain a colony here', we told ourselves, 'They will send us money and men, then our situation will be good. If they don't want to do that, they will find a way, in their wisdom and strength, to withdraw with glory the remains of an army composed of the elite warriors of France.'

Alas, neither of the two alternatives was really considered. We were left to our own resources and if merely a quarter of this army finally returned to its native land, it was due rather to a happy combination of circumstances than to any particular care or attention on the part of the Government.

Having enlightened us by means of his proclamations, the Commanding General started his programme of action by recalling us to Cairo. So we left Salheyeh on 22nd Messidor [11th July 1800] and arrived on 23rd at Cueta, a little town on the Delta where, as we passed through, we visited the tomb of Mohammed's father-in-law, rather from curiosity than devotion to Mohammedanism, as you will appreciate.

The tomb is famous in that country, and is one of its most handsome monuments. It is located in a huge and wealthy mosque. The doors of the mosque are covered in silver plates, and the interior is lit by many lamps of the same metal. The tomb itself can be a substitute for that of the Prophet himself. Such Muslims as are unable to travel to Mecca go on pilgrimage to Ceuta, as Spaniards who cannot go to Rome journey instead to St James of Compostella. All good followers of Mohammed should, at some time in their life, visit at least one of these two shrines if they hope to achieve an exalted place in the Paradise of Delights.

We reached Cairo on 26th Messidor [15th July 1800] and took up garrison duty until the 8th Thermidor [27th July 1800] when the second battalion of the 75th arrived at Gizeh.

Although we had, at first, felt some prejudice against General Menou as a result of his change of name and his affection for Egypt, we soon came to appreciate his excellent qualities, his orderliness and economy, his care for the soldiers and his great knowledge of administration as well as his moral virtues. Understanding the human heart so well, he sought to lead us by persuasion rather than by the severity of his orders; he could, however, be firm when required, as an example which will be recounted shortly will show.

He was always accessible and friendly and did everything in his power for the servicemen, no matter how low in rank. It was clear from his polished manners that he had been well educated and came from a good background. He suppressed the leeches of the army, and the administrators who enriched themselves at our expense, and managed, by his determination, quickly to root out several intolerable abuses. He surrounded himself with advisers and with all those who might help in his management of affairs. On 15th Fructidor, Year VIII [2nd September 1800] he set up what was called the Privy Council of Egypt which was composed of several former high-ranking officers. This Council was informed of all civil matters, commerce, agriculture, finance, science and the arts etc., everything except war and foreign policy. On all these latter subjects the General reserved to himself the right to reject, to approve, or to alter. Although the Council caused him some annoyance, through rivalry, or the spirit of contradiction which existed in some of its members, he nevertheless won the respect of most of the military; and, as a man of character, silenced rumour and did not hesitate to call attention to excess, as we shall see.

Headquarters, Cairo, 18th Fructidor, Year VIII [5th September 1800]
Menou, Commanding General, to the Army

Soldiers,
I have promised always to tell you the truth. I shall keep my word. I am dissatisfied with many of you. Serious complaints have been made; crimes are being committed, soldiers are treating the native people outrageously. What is the matter with you? You are Republicans, and yet are not civilised! You are Frenchmen, yet you behave like the barbarians. Ah! I should like to believe that the excesses which have been committed by so many of you are only the results of drunkenness. But, soldiers, is not this drunkenness capable of anything? The drunken man is frenzied, he can abandon himself to any excess, and commit the most dreadful crimes. Do you really wish to

resemble the barbarians whom you reduced to dust on the plains of Heliopolis and Matarieh!

Soldiers, the greatest man of antiquity, Alexander the Great, who conquered Egypt, nevertheless, in the opinion of thoughtful men, lost most of his reputation because of the excesses he committed in drunken rages; and this great conqueror would have been nothing but a scourge of humanity had he not been able, through noble actions, to redeem some of the crimes he had committed.

Soldiers, learn to be charitable to the Egyptians; but, what am I saying? Today the Egyptians are Frenchmen: they are your brothers. Learn to respect old age, learn to respect women, learn to be just. What glory can you earn by ill-treating a man who trembles before you as you insult or violate his wife? Treat him, then, as you would wish to be treated if you were in his place and he in yours. Generals, commanding officers, officers of all ranks, repeat these words continually to all the troops under your command. Tell them that, though they compel me to enforce severe discipline, yet I am more distressed than those I punish; tell them that I seek day and night to ensure their well-being; they owe it to me, and owe it even more to their own honour, to behave like true, like noble Republicans.

Complaints have also reached me about offences committed in the public baths. Men have wanted to take women there and to bathe with them. In all law-abiding countries this offence is condemned. It destroys public morals; it is anti-social. I therefore order all Generals, military commanders of any rank, to suppress and punish with the utmost severity all the above mentioned crimes.

Menou.

Our General had promised us to tell us of the news he received from France. The following will show how sincerely he kept his word.

Headquarters, Cairo, Menou, Commanding General, to the Army

I have just learned that a ship from France has reached the port of Alexandria. French armies are victorious. A battle such has never before been recorded in history has made us masters of Italy. Bonaparte, in person, was in command. There has been a similar success on the Rhine. In the Vendée, the people of these previously rebellious provinces have repelled the English who had attempted a raid. The government is respected and obeyed. Everywhere, confidence has been so restored that the economy is in excellent condition.

As further details reach me I shall pass them on to the army.

Menou.

When we learned the details of the battle of Marengo we found that our forces had gathered new laurels, and that the surrender of several forts by the Austrians had placed us again in command of a country which had been lost to us through incompetence or treason. This news was all the more welcome to the Army of Egypt which had been recruited almost exclusively from the army which had conquered Italy with so much toil and suffering. It is noticeable that the ordinary soldier loves his conquests with as much, perhaps even more, ardour, than is felt by the heads of government. Our joy would have been more complete if we had not heard of the death of General Desaix,[91] who had so recently left us, and who was still one of the idols of our affection and respect.

On the first day of Vendémiaire, Year IX [23rd September 1800], General Menou caused us to be paid all our arrears, bringing our pay up to date and ensuring it for the future. He had achieved this remarkable result by means of careful administration, methods which, while mindful of the well-being of the Army, did not forget the interests of the inhabitants of the country or oppress them. His worst enemies themselves were forced to pay tribute to his administrative skill and the unfailing care he devoted to improving the lot of the soldiers.

If providence had decided to permit us to set up a colony in Egypt, no one would have been more capable than he [Menou] of bringing it to prosperity and stability, but, sadly, it seemed that this unhappy country, once so rich and enlightened, was condemned to barbarism, misery and the most appalling superstition for ages to come.

---

[91] General Desaix was killed at the battle of Marengo (see Short Biographies).

CHAPTER XI

On the 15th Vendémiaire [7th October 1800], our second battalion left
Gizeh and rejoined the demi-brigade at Cairo. On the 18th it embarked at
Bulaq to go to Alexandria where it arrived on the 23rd of the same month. I
did not at that time know that I had left forever the great city of Cairo, the
pyramids and everything pleasant in Egypt. I bade them farewell only from
afar, and nothing but memories remain to me. It was at Alexandria that the
following news reached us.

> Headquarters, Cairo, 15th Brumaire, Year IX [6th November 1800]
> Menou, Commanding General, to the army

> The Commander-in-Chief has already mentioned that the escort vessel *San-
> Philippo*, having left Toulon on 15th Vendémiaire, arrived in the port of
> Alexandria on 9th Brumaire [31st October 1800], carrying dispatches from
> the government. The following is a letter written by the First Consul to the
> heads of Departments.

(This letter, which is not included here, dealt with the negotiations at
Lunéville,[92] where it was resolved that the Austrian Emperor would
negotiate separately if England would not agree to the terms, and proposals
on the part of the French Government to pursue the national interest
vigorously.)

---

[92] The treaty of Lunéville which forced the Austrian Emperor to accept Bonaparte's
terms was not signed until 9th February 1801, after the battle of Hohenlinden. It
effectively reorganised what had been the Holy Roman Empire and made Bonaparte
the arbiter of German territory.

Let us then continue with matters that concern us more closely.

A letter from Commandant Carnot,[93] Minister of War, to General Abd. J. Menou, Commander-in- Chief of the Army of the East, 23rd Fructidor, Year VIII [10th September 1800]

The Government has read, with the greatest interest, all the information contained in your despatch and, with confidence in your ability and devotion to the cause of maintaining and increasing the prosperity of this important conquest, hereby confirms you as Commander of the brave army which has twice conquered that land and defends it with such courage.

I send you herewith the warrant of your rank and that of those officers whose outstanding services, as well as the recommendation of General Kléber, have caused them to be promoted to higher rank.

The First Consul has hastened to confirm these recommendations in order to bestow on the Army of the East and its worthy leaders a further sign of the satisfaction that the entire Republic feels in their labour, their determination and their glory. The time may not be far off, perhaps, when the army will earn an even greater prize. They may see the English, those violators of treaties, forced by the indomitable courage of those same heroes whose shame and ruin they had the insolence to propose, tremble for themselves and submit at last to the honourable and moderate conditions which France triumphant offers for the peace of Europe.

You will hasten this longed-for moment, Citizen General, if you follow in the footsteps of your predecessors, by strengthening with unwavering firmness and perfecting by all means in your power, the foundations laid for the preservation and prosperity of Egypt, until a comprehensive peace shall finally decide the future of this momentous and precious conquest.

Rest assured that the Government will neglect nothing that can be of help to the Army of the East. It is the object of their constant solicitude.
Carnot.

Army of the East, you perceive how concerned the Government is about you, you understand how important Egypt is in the balance of political power, you see how your courage and success attracts the admiration of Europe; you deserve the gratitude of the nation.

I have sent word to the First Consul that he can count upon your complete devotion and upon my unwavering resolution. Soldiers, I repeat once more that I shall persist in my care for all that can help to improve your lot; but also, I expect in return your complete confidence, discipline, obedience and submission. Bear in mind that I have continually to reconcile the interests of the Central Government, the Army and that of the Egyptian people, whose government is in my hands.

---

[93] Lazare Nicolas Marguerite Carnot (1753–1823), Count from 1815. One of the most influential figures of the period; known as 'the organiser of victory'.

Remember that, in order to achieve this aim, I must, even as I extract from Egypt all the wealth it is capable of supplying, work for the well-being of the people who live there; I must win their confidence by good treatment; they must quickly learn to appreciate the difference between their old rulers and the Government of the French Republic. In a word, firmness, humanity, morality and honesty must govern all my actions. I shall try to provide you with an example. To do this I have only to follow in the footsteps of Bonaparte.
Menou.

The victories won by our arms in Europe seemed to auger the triumph of the Republic and our army was overjoyed. But it was cast down by the news of the fall of Malta. Even as the first news had given us hope, so did the latter news make us fear that it would be impossible for us to return to our homeland. The English, filled with pride at their new triumph, so we told ourselves, would no longer wish to agree to any treaty. This was more or less the general opinion. But, having thought of these things, we permitted ourselves a vague hope which lingered in our unhappy hearts, and enabled us to await the uncertain future with more courage. It seemed to us that the conclusion of a general peace presented no insoluble problems, and this thought sustained us. It is true that hostilities had started again. But General Moreau[94] had, on one front, won a considerable victory on the Rhine, where he had made (...)[95] men prisoner of war, taken eighty cannon and two hundred ammunition wagons and, on another front, a formidable army had marched into Italy and already seized Tuscany. Everywhere our troops were doing well, but all these successes, brilliant though they were, did nothing to improve our situation in Egypt. We received no reinforcements; our army dwindled daily through illness and a thousand other minor accidents. It was not difficult to foresee that we might soon be thrown out. We were threatened by a large Turkish army, and an assault by the English. Although one's resolve is normally stiffened by blows of fate, yet we became apathetic, indifferent to everything, even to life itself, though we resolved to sell it dearly should anyone attack us. We waited only for the outcome and the passage of time.

On the 1st Ventôse, Year IX [20th February 1801] our second battalion left Alexandria and arrived on the 2nd at a mosque which stood between the sea and Elko, where all night long it endured a terrible storm and tempest, which seemed to presage some dreadful catastrophe to us. On the 3rd we

---

[94] Jean Victor Marie Moreau (1763–1813); one of the most able French generals of the period, banished by Napoleon and mortally wounded at Dresden while serving as military adviser to the Tsar.
[95] No number is given in the original text.

arrived at Rosetta, where the health administrators advised us of some unusual precautions to be taken against the plague. On the 5th we were at El Ramanieh. On the 11th there was a new sighting of the English fleet off Alexandria. Then a surprise. An order to leave at once was given and obeyed immediately. On the same day we found ourselves back at the mosque, and on the 13th at the headquarters at Elko. We left once more in the evening of the 15th. Circumstances then dictated various movements which were so numerous as to be impossible – as well as pointless – to itemise.

On the 17th Ventôse [8th March 1801], at ten o'clock in the morning, the English disembarked at Aboukir. They were opposed, but the advantage remained with the most numerous: the French retreated to the heights above Rosetta on the sea.

On the 21st [12th March 1801] the enemy made a move; we hurried to meet them and to impede their progress.

On the 28th [19th March 1801][96] the English attacked in three columns; the French swooped down on them, fighting desperately and achieving wonders despite their numerical inferiority, but were finally forced to give way after inflicting great damage, and retreated to the heights above Rosetta port.

On the 29th [20th March 1801] the army arrived from Cairo and attacked at dawn on the 30th, but the English had set up impenetrable defences, through which it was impossible to break; many attacks were made, all were futile. Every trick of war was tried, every effort made, but retreat was inevitable with great loss on both sides. Instead of retreating, the question of a second attack had been discussed; after many arguments for and against, it was decided that the army should return to Cairo and place itself on the defensive. We had, it was argued, very good positions there, and the English had none. If they wanted to obtain them they would have to be won at the point of the sword. One is stronger in defence than in attack and this was the course of action which was chosen; that is to say that one part of the army would return to Cairo, and the other – in which I was – would remain in Lower Egypt.

A few days later, the dissension which had existed for a long while between the Commanding General and several of the Generals of Division took on a character which threatened the confidence and peace of mind of the army. Vigorous discussions had taken place between the two parties and comments injurious to the General had been made. Weary of this oppo-

---

[96] This date for the British attack may be an error. An action of this type (attack 'in three columns'), sometimes styled *Mandora*, took place on 13th March 1801; other sources refer to no action on 19th March.

sition, he made up his mind to resolve matters by exerting his authority; the arrest was made at night and without warning, of Generals Reynier and Damas, *Adjudant-Général* Boyer,[97] Inspector of Revenue Daure and several of their supporters. They were put on board ship and sent to France. This prompt action produced conflicting opinions among the soldiers. Some approved of the punishment of the generals, 'It was they', it was said, 'who had been responsible for the failure of the attack on the 30th'. Some added that they were about to betray us, or had already betrayed us. Others, more moderate, accused them only of lack of respect and disobedience to the Commander-in-Chief. The opposition to these views maintained that the Commanding General was overbearing and lacked foresight; they charged him with a stubborn insistence on retaining the colony. Those who were most reasonable, in my view, were those who left it to the Government to decide such matters and simply carried out their duties.

During March and April the English seized Rosetta and breached the dyke on Lake Madieh. The waters flooded in all directions and soon reached Lake Mareotis. This new sea increased to such an extent that during May the English were able to move armed barks around on it; we did the same and there were several little battles, in which we were often victorious.

On the 19th Floréal [9th May 1801] there was a battle at El Rahmanieh, following which we evacuated the place on the night of 19th–20th.

On the 20th Prairial [9th June 1801] the corvette *Heliopolis* arrived in the ancient port of Alexandria, bringing us news of reinforcements under Admiral Ganteaume, for which we waited in vain.

On the 30th [19th June 1801] the Regiment of Dromedaries rejoined us and brought us reassuring news from Cairo. On 11th Messidor [29th June 1801] there was an artillery salvo from all the forts and along the whole front to mark the anniversary of the taking of Alexandria; this was for the last time.

On the 20th Messidor [9th July 1801] the English negotiated and informed us of the surrender of the troops stationed in Cairo and the adjoining forts. We should not have believed it unless it had been confirmed by the following proclamation:

General Headquarters, Alexandria, 20th Messidor [9th July 1801]
Commanding General, Army of the East, beneath the walls of Alexandria

Generals, officers, non-commissioned officers and men of the army,
The French troops who were in Cairo and the forts around it have surren-

---

[97] Pierre François Joseph Boyer (1772–1851), Baron from 1812.

dered without a fight, and without either the town or the forts having been seriously attacked. I will not permit myself to comment at all on this occurrence, possibly the most extraordinary to happen in war, for I fear to heap dishonour men on who, until now, had shown themselves worthy of the names of Frenchmen and Republicans.

I have to tell you that I have here with me Lieutenants General Friant and Rampon,[98] Generals of Division Songis,[99] Destaing,[100] Zayonchek[101] and General of Brigade Sanson, Commander of the Engineers. All have been of the opinion that we must behave like men whose only rules of conduct are those of honour and devotion to the fatherland.

Soldiers, you have always shown such devotion, such patience and such courage that I shall not insult you by questioning for one moment your future behaviour; we shall show what can be done by brave soldiers, we shall defend ourselves to the death. But if there are amongst us, and among other Frenchmen here, those who lack the endurance to fight any longer against the enemies of the Republic, then the door is open for them: I will send them to Rosetta, when within a few days they may join up with the troops coming down from Cairo.

Menou.

This proclamation and many others of the same type, all proclaiming honour and duty, nevertheless did not please the soldiers, who felt that it ruled out any hope of a treaty and a return to France. They were jealous of their comrades in arms who, before their eyes, were setting sail for their homeland, while they saw themselves surrounded in Alexandria, exposed to all the dangers of a siege and the horrors of hunger. It was, in fact, all that this town, cut off from communication with the rest of Egypt, offered to its inhabitants and its defenders. A ration of bad, salty bread, a few handfuls of rice or lentils, sometimes six ounces of meat and this only for a while, such was the daily provision for each man. The Bedouins came, however, to sell us a little corn, but this always cost its weight in gold. We could hardly manage to buy any meat, even of camel, donkey or horse. If, to this suffering, is added continual labour, endless duties, lack of money, innumerable illnesses for which, without medicine, there was no cure, then one would have some idea of our wretched situation. Ah, well, if there were some grumbles and some complaints, honour caused them to die on the lips and courage and the determination to make even greater sacrifices were reawakened.

For five months the two armies confronted each other near Alexandria,

---

[98] Antoine Guillaume Rampon (1759–1842), Count from 1808.
[99] Nicolas Marie Songis des Courbons (1761–1810), Count from 1809.
[100] Jacques Zacharie Destaing (1764–1802); killed in a duel with Reynier.
[101] Joseph Zayonchek (1762–1826).

without any military move being made by either side, because at first the English were engaged by the Army of Cairo and the French were too few in numbers to attack. The departure of our comrades who had been in Cairo allowed our enemies to gather their forces against us. They began, towards the end of Thermidor (July/August), to send an amazing number of small boats and armed sloops across Lake Madieh and Lake Mareotis to be at hand for a landing near the city, which skilfully constructed earthworks had rendered inaccessible.

On the 29th Thermidor [17th August 1801] they actually attacked our lines and seized a favourable position on our left, from which our troops cleared them soon afterwards. We were not equally successful on our right where the enemy captured an advanced redoubt from us which then became a threat to our line. A battalion and two companies of grenadiers tried to retake it, but their efforts failed. On the same day the enemy succeeded in landing a large number of troops near Marabout, which we were unable to prevent.

In the evening of the 30th Thermidor, the second battalion of the 75th moved to the redoubts of Pompey, so called because they were near Pompey's column.

On the 4th Fructidor [21st August 1801], in the morning, the enemy seized the fort of Marabout, after a heavy bombardment which lasted three days and established a line from their point of disembarkation up to the heights surrounding the Turkish fort. This caused us a great deal of trouble.

On the 7th [24th August 1801] they attacked and took possession of several hillocks which were nearest to the Turkish fort, after having taken prisoner a battalion of the 18th, most of whom managed to escape under cover of night.

On the 8th our lines before the port of Rosetta were subjected to cannon fire, bombarded and sustained a great deal of damage, while disturbing preparations were made on our right flank which made us fear for the future. We decided to ask for a truce for a few days, and this was granted to us on the night of the 8th/9th Fructidor.

On the 12th, in the evening, a surrender was agreed, which was ratified on the 14th and 15th, under which we gave up the two lines and the triangular fort, and we retreated into the compound which was named 'of the Arabs'. The English undertook to convey us back to French territory. This surrender was signed by Menou and by the English General, Hutchinson. Our embarkation was to take place on the tenth day following the ratification, that is to say on 25th Fructidor year IX [12th September 1801].

Unforeseen circumstances compelled the English to use the ships on which we should have embarked to take troops to different parts of Europe as their own affairs required. So, instead of leaving in a single convoy, we embarked progressively as our ships were repaired, so that a month later we were still in Egypt. Postponed from one day to another, we should have embarked at last on the first day of Vendémiaire, Year X [23rd September 1801], but the lethargy of the Commander-in-Chief (a fault which was unusual in him) held us up for a further eight days. We finally set sail on 20th Vendémiaire [12th October], a day for which we had so long and so fervently wished. It was forty-eight days after the ratification of the surrender.

Our ship was a merchantman called the *Sacre Famiglia*. We rejoiced to leave a country so disastrous for the French now and in the past, a country scourged by all the afflictions of humanity, plague, blindness, banditry, poverty and, above all, by Oriental despotism, but we grieved for the many men we had lost, the quantity of blood that had been spilled, the toil and privations we had suffered, without having founded a colony such as would have made up for much. But the time for her rebirth had not yet dawned for Egypt.

For my own part, I very much regretted my beloved and unhappy Zulima. Only the sight of my country could heal the wound and soothe the sorrow inflicted by her loss. I had written her a letter from Rosetta, after the surrender of Cairo, in which I bid her, when she heard talk of our surrender to the English, to try to come and join me at Alexandria, so that she could leave with us for France. She actually escaped from Damiette on the 25th Fructidor [12th September 1801], dressed in the French style and with her faithful maid, but she was stopped on the road by a party of Mameluks, who, having questioned her, realised from her speech that she was not French and, seeing that she was very lovely, kept her in slavery, while letting her maid, who came from Marseilles, go free, as being one of our countrywomen and so included in the terms of surrender. I do not know what became of Zulima. Perhaps she died of misery? I learned these details from her maid who embarked with us and had the happiness of being reunited with her parents and her home in Marseilles.

During the early days of our voyage, unfavourable winds made our journey slow. On the sixth day a completely contrary wind gave us great trouble and halted our progress. It was not until the 29th that we finally doubled the Cape St Jean (off the island of Candie). After that, Aeolus, growing kinder, filled our sails and pushed us towards the coast of Sicily, between Cape Murro di Porco and La Vignette, near Syracuse, and there abandoned us to a complete calm, so that we were in the greatest danger. Far from escaping from this trap, we seemed to be about to be cast up on the shore. Our sailors lost their heads and, having consulted their charts, saw no other way out of the difficulty than to land at La Vignette. They then tried their best, but in vain, to lower the anchor in an anchorage which offered little security, but even as they struggled a soft breeze rose, which carried us from this unfortunate situation. We had hardly rounded the Cape Murro di Porco before our older sailors, who had known this part of the world for forty or fifty years, gave vent to their joy and relief. They said they had never before been in such great danger.

On the same day, we were forced to drop anchor at Augusta, a little town in Sicily, both to repair damage and to await the favourable weather, which we should need in order to pass through the dangerous Straits of Messina. The governor of the town made us welcome, but enforced the usual health precautions. By indirect means we learned that a peace between the French Republic and the Court of St James had been signed.

We left Augusta on the 4th Brumaire [26th October 1801], but without a favourable wind made little headway.

On the 5th we remained the whole day becalmed at the foot of Mount Etna, which continually emitted a thick, sulphurous smoke from its high crater. During the night we could sometimes see fiery particles coming from the summit and falling on the pleasant countryside and the houses around. On the night of the 5th/6th Brumaire the breeze freshened and we were able, at last, to continue on our way. By moonlight we saw the town of Messina. It lies by the sea at the foot of a range of volcanic mountains, and presents a delightful prospect.

Next we attempted the passage of the straits between Calabria and Sicily. In this strait between Scylla and Charybdis, so dreaded and so famous in antiquity, is what is now known as the Lighthouse of Messina. The darkness of night made it impossible for us to see anything at all. The wind had dropped during the 6th so that we remained becalmed opposite Stromboli. This is a mountain in the middle of the sea, forty miles from the Lighthouse. It is even more famous than Etna (from which it is separated by many islands, chiefly Vulcano and Lipari) by reason of the flow of lava and the bellowing sounds it emits. When night fell, a storm or tempest arose which continued until morning and caused us much suffering. The captain of the ship considered that it was impossible to remain at sea without risking being crushed against one of the rocks at the foot of Stromboli. Therefore, on the morning of 7th he took the decision to return through the straits. Thus I was able to see, near Calabria, a mountain, part of which had previously overhung the sea, and which had fallen into it during the earthquakes of 1782 and 1783. It appears that this was where Scylla and her barking dogs[102] had been. As for Charybdis, I saw nothing

---

[102] Scylla's lower body was supposed to be composed of the heads of ferocious dogs, each of which would bite off the head of any seaman unlucky enough to come near.

on the coast opposite Sicily that resembled the classic descriptions. It is true that, peering deeper, I could make out a contrast in the path of the swirling waters, such as might have been a hazard to navigation, given that there was so little room to manoeuvre.

I observed, along the shores at the feet of the opposing mountains, fertile, well-cultivated hillsides, handsome country houses and well-built villages; altogether a delightful sight.

At midday we arrived at Messina and anchored to await a favourable wind; we found there several ships which had left Alexandria several days before us; this encounter consoled us a little for our ill-luck. While there I saw the remains of the magnificent houses which had adorned the port and formed, so to speak, its immense outline before the earthquake which had engulfed the unhappy town in 1782. The inhabitants had rebuilt, bit by bit, behind the row of ruins, which no doubt they had dared not restore for fear of a new disaster.

The new buildings were very unlike the old ones. They were only two stories high and of less elegant construction. Shortly after our arrival the Governor of Messina sent musicians to entertain us; we gave them money and they were so well pleased with our generosity that they returned the following day. We rewarded them again in the same way and they would have returned every day if our stay in that place had been prolonged, for the Sicilians, even more than other Italians, are so importunate that they have no shame about continually holding out their hands.

It was in that town that we received confirmation and details of the peace signed between France and England. We stayed there until the 14th and set sail on that day. A calm sea welcomed us and we again passed Stromboli on the evening of the 15th; a favourable wind which then rose blew us, on the evening of the 19th, into the Toulon Roads.

We were hoping to end to our travels where they had begun three years earlier; but an order from higher up sent us on to Marseilles. It seemed that France had some difficulty in receiving us. We were unable to leave until the 22nd.

Arriving at the port of Marseilles at nine in the evening we were met by a contrary wind and dreadful weather, which blew us out to sea. A distress signal was fired. A pilot arrived and guided us to a very poor anchorage where we were not at all comfortable. We raised anchor on the 24th in order to move into the quarantine area. On the 25th Brumaire, Year X [16th November 1801], we finally went into quarantine in berth nine.

When quarantine ended, our beloved country took us, at last, into her arms.

SHORT BIOGRAPHIES

SHORT BIOGRAPHIES

Eugène Rose de Beauharnais, Viceroy of Italy (1781–1824)

Of all the splendid figures of the Napoleonic era, vying for power, becoming rulers of new kingdoms and dukedoms, earning wealth and fame on the battlefield, Eugène de Beauharnais is perhaps one of the most extraordinary. His descendants are now on the thrones of Sweden, Norway, Denmark and Belgium, a distinction shared only with Marshal Bernadotte.

Nothing in his early life foreshadowed what was to come. His mother, Rose Tascher de la Pagerie, the daughter of a sugar planter in the French colony of Martinique, had been sent to Paris in 1779 to become the bride of Alexandre de Beauharnais. Alexandre, who was serving as an officer in the Republican Army at the time of its most severe reverses in 1793, was blamed for the fall of Mainz to the advancing allies. He was arrested and by the time his son Eugène was 14 years old his father had been guillotined and his mother was in prison expecting a similar fate, having been denounced as the '*ci-devant Vicomtess de Beauharnais*'.

Rose Beauharnais was saved by the fall of Robespierre and on her release she exploited her beauty and charm, as well as the friends she had made in the prison of La Chaumière, to the full. One of her conquests was General Hoche, whose admiration was such that he appointed the youthful Eugène as one of his aides. It was a post that he would again fill when Napoleon Bonaparte became his step-father. He served as General Bonaparte's aide-de-camp during the closing year of the Italian campaign and accompanied Napoleon on the Egyptian expedition. He was one of the two officers sent under a flag of truce to obtain the surrender of the garrison of Jaffa; the terms on which this was obtained were later dishonoured by Napoleon. In a failed assault on Acre, Beauharnais was one of a storming party of which every member was either killed or wounded.

When Napoleon deserted his army and returned to France in August 1799, Eugène was one of the few to accompany him, shortly afterwards being promoted and given the command of the Light Cavalry of the Consular Guard.

In the course of the second Italian campaign, Eugène de Beauharnais distinguished himself at Marengo in 1800. In the succeeding years, which were those in which his step-father rose to unprecedented power, Beauharnais enjoyed to the full the pleasures and luxuries of his mother's home at Malmaison. When Napoleon was declared Emperor of the French in 1804, Beauharnais was promoted to General and made a Prince of the Empire in the following year. Further honours came to him when his step-father assumed the crown of Lombardy in 1805; Eugène was proclaimed Viceroy of Italy – he was 24 years old. Pursuing Napoleon's instructions he organised an army, introduced a civil code, and built canals, fortifications and schools. He was soon to be put in command of the Army of Italy in Massena's[103] place, but in 1806 he was summoned in haste to Munich where his marriage to Auguste-Amélie, the daughter of the King of Bavaria, had been arranged. This further evidence of his compliance with his step-father's will was acknowledged by his formal adoption as a son by Bona-parte. The marriage, though diplomatic in intent, was a happy one.

In 1809 the Kingdom of Italy was threatened by an Austrian attempt to regain their old territory, and Eugène's army, reinforced by General Macdonald[104], succeeded in repelling the invasion after an initial defeat. Thereafter both commanders served with distinction at Wagram.

Beauharnais gave an even more positive indication of his support for his adoptive father when he helped to convince his mother, now the Empress Josephine, to agree to her divorce from Napoleon. Is it possible that he thought that he might be named heir to the still childless Emperor? Meanwhile the government of his heterogeneous kingdom occupied his time fully, for he was seen there as Napoleon's puppet and faced numerous challenges to his regime, which he succeeded in overcoming.

In 1812 Prince Eugène with an army of forty thousand men and five thousand horses commanded IV Corps of the Grand Army in the Russian campaign, taking a leading part in the battles of Smolensk and Borodino. In the dreadful retreat from Moscow in December 1812, the prince, together with Murat, formed the rear guard, eventually finding himself in command of the remains of the army, struggling to return to France.

He remained loyal to the Emperor, organising a defence of Italy against the Austrians, but it was a rear-guard action and when Napoleon abdicated in 1814 Eugène was forced to come to terms with the allies and he returned to Munich to await their decision as to his fate. On the return of the Emperor from Elba, Eugène did not join him, prevented by a promise he had given to the allies. He was made Duke of Leuchtenberg and Prince of Eichstadt by his father-in-law and lived out his life in Munich, where he was much concerned with the welfare of old soldiers, relics of the years of warfare. He

---

[103] André Massena (1758–1817), Marshal from 1804, Duke of Rivoli, Prince of Essling.
[104] Jacques Etienne Joseph Alexandre Macdonald (1765–1840), later Duke of Tarentum.

died of apoplexy in 1824 when only 43 years old. His daughter Josephine married Oscar the First, King of Sweden, the son of Marshal Bernadotte.

General Louis Charles Desaix, Chevalier de Veygoux (1768–1800)

This distinguished soldier came from a noble family. He left the military school of Effiat when he was 15 years old, holding the rank of sub-lieutenant. When the Revolution started, he was a lieutenant in a regiment in Brittany and he did not emigrate, unlike his aristocratic family, with whom he quarrelled. He rose in rank, serving with the Army of the Rhine. His bravery in combat, where he was wounded several times, enabled him to escape the persecution that his emigré parents had experienced. By 1794 he was a General of Division and continued to serve with great distinction, transferring in 1797 to the Army of Italy under the command of Napoleon Bonaparte.

In 1798 Desaix accompanied Napoleon on the expedition to Egypt, leading the 1st Division at the Battle of the Pyramids and pursuing the Mameluk leader, Murad Bey, into Upper Egypt. He was appointed Governor of Upper Egypt, a role that involved continual battles and skirmishes, and in which his skill both as a soldier and as an administrator was amply demonstrated. Desaix was one of the signatories of the Convention of El Arich, the failed agreement between the English, the Turks and the French. Shortly afterwards he attempted to return to France, but his ship was captured by the Royal Navy, who interned him at Livorno. He was, however, released in time to join Napoleon at the battle of Marengo, where he was able to mount a last minute counter-attack, having returned to the battle in defiance of his orders, thereby turning probable defeat into victory for the French. Napoleon's reputation was saved, but Desaix was killed, shot in the heart at the start of the final charge.

Ahmed Djezzar Pasha (1735–1804)

Djezzar was born a Christian in 1735, in Bosnia. Ferocious from an early age, he fled from his crimes to Cairo and, converting to Islam, became the servant, perhaps the slave, of a Mameluk who employed him to gather taxes. He amassed wealth and power for himself, becoming widely feared for his brutality and earning the name of 'The Butcher'. When he finally quarrelled with his patron he fled into Syria where the Turks appointed him governor of Acre. From the crumbling fortifications of this city he wielded influence over a huge province, ruling as a virtual king, never hesitating to have the Sultan's emissaries slaughtered if he did not like the instructions they brought.

When Napoleon Bonaparte invaded Syria to repel the Turkish Army, then preparing to contest his conquest of Egypt, Djezzar and his troops presented the first true opposition. With the dreadful knowledge of the French massacre of their countrymen at Jaffa fresh in their minds, the Turks under Djezzar put up an obstinate resistance to the French siege of Acre, assisted by English gunners and the lively help of Admiral Sir Sidney Smith and the guns of his ships, and forced the French to retreat without capturing the city. It was during this siege that Djezzar, taking advantage of the temporary absence of the British Admiral at sea, brutally avenged the French massacre of Turkish troops by tying French prisoners together in pairs, enclosing them in sacks and casting them into the sea.

The capitulation of the French in Egypt in the year 1801, and the eventual withdrawal of the British, permitted the Grand Vizier to regain control of the region and massacre the remaining Mameluk Beys. Syria also came under effective Turkish rule when Djezzar died in 1804.

Ibrahim Bey, Emir of Egypt (1735–1817)

Ibrahim was born in Europe, but was sold as a slave to the Mameluk Abu Dahab; on his master's death he became joint ruler of Egypt with Murad Bey. Following the Battle of the Pyramids, where he fought with stubborn skill, he was compelled to flee into Syria and continued his opposition to the invading French, fighting them once more at Heliopolis. However, following the evacuation of Egypt by the French, Ibrahim did not regain power, although he avoided the massacre of the Mameluks which took place in 1811.

Admiral George Keith Elphinstone, Viscount (1746–1823)

The second son of Lord Elphinstone, Keith was born at Elphinstone Tower, Stirling. His long career in the Royal Navy began at the age of fifteen when he went on board the *Gosport*, a ship of forty-four guns under the command of Captain John Jervis, later to become Earl St Vincent. In 1767 he embarked on a private venture to China in an East India Company ship commanded by his brother William. This expedition was such a commercial success that it ensured his financial independence. He achieved the rank of lieutenant in the Royal Navy in 1770 and was actively employed in various ships in the Mediterranean and on convoy duty to Newfoundland. He became a post-captain in 1775, when his duties in enforcing the blockade of the North American colonies led to his serving with distinction on land at the reduction of Charleston. In 1780, on his return to Britain, he became Member of Parliament for Dumbarton, and in 1787 married Jane Mercer.

Keith did not apply for another ship until war with France appeared imminent, and in 1793 he was appointed to command the seventy-four-gun *Robust*, in which he sailed for the Mediterranean with Lord Hood. He took a prominent part in the capture of Toulon, finding his previous military experience at Charleston of great value. When the British occupation of Toulon came to an end it was due in considerable part to his skill that thousands of troops and Royalist fugitives were safely re-embarked and were spared the Terror which broke out in the town afterwards.

Keith was promoted to rear-admiral in 1794 and in 1795 went as commander-in-chief of an expedition to the Cape of Good Hope where his service against the Dutch brought sufficient prize money to make him a wealthy man. He was created an Irish peer, Baron Keith of Stonehaven and Marischal, in 1797, when the suppression of the Sheerness mutiny was largely due to his efforts. A stern disciplinarian, held in respect in the Navy, he was also able to quell disaffection among the Plymouth sailors.

A long period of action and frustration followed his departure for the Mediterranean, under the command of Earl St Vincent, where he pursued a French fleet that eluded him from the Mediterranean to Brest. In 1799 he entered the harbour of Genoa, which he had blockaded, in cooperation with an Austrian land force.

Poor communications between the various units of the Mediterranean command, as well as with the Government in Britain, led to the unfortunate repudiation by Lord Keith of a Convention which would have ended the war in Egypt. This led to accusations of bad faith and the renewal of hostilities, which were ended by the arrival in Egypt of a British force under General Abercromby, escorted by a naval contingent commanded by Admiral Lord Keith.

Following his return to England, Keith received many acknowledgements of his service, being made a freeman of London and a peer of the United Kingdom, as well as being awarded the order of the Crescent by the Sultan. On the fresh outbreak of war with France he was appointed Commander-in-Chief in the North Sea from 1803 until 1807. His wife having died some years earlier, he married Hester Maria, a daughter of Dr Johnson's friend, Mrs Thrale. The second Lady Keith was no longer young but was undoubtedly learned, having studied 'perspective, fortifications, Hebrew and mathematics'.

On 31st July 1815, Lord Keith had the unenviable task of going on board the *Bellerophon* in Plymouth Sound to inform Napoleon of the Government's decision to exile him to St Helena. This was the Admiral's last action as a serving officer. He retired to his estate at Tulliallan after no less than fifty-three years with the Royal Navy, nearly all of it spent on active service.

His long career encompassed the whole of the French revolutionary and

Napoleonic wars, which has directed the spotlight of history upon his actions. He seems to have been steady, brave and cautious, qualities which avoided the commission of serious mistakes, but which leave the impression of a commander who was good rather than great.

He died at Tulliallan on 10th March 1823, aged 76.

Jean Baptiste Kléber (1753–1800)

Kléber was born at Strasbourg in 1753. He was originally an architect, but preferred a military profession and entered into the Austrian service in 1777. Unable to attain a higher rank than that of lieutenant, he returned to Alsace in 1785, where he became an inspector of public buildings, joining the National Guard in 1789. He made rapid progress and in 1792 was a lieutenant colonel in a volunteer regiment.

He displayed great skill and bravery at the siege of Mainz in 1793, after which he served in the Vendée, but the bloody scenes there so disgusted him that he obtained his recall and was engaged in the north, where he defeated the Austrians, took Mons and drove the enemy from Louvaine. He also captured Maastricht and contributed to the successes of the campaigns of 1795 and 1796. Under the Directory he was given the command of the Army of the Sambre and Meuse, which he later resigned to Hoche. Feeling that he had not shared in the honours showered on Moreau and Pichegru, he accepted no further offers of command until Napoleon, well aware of his qualities, persuaded him to take command of a division in the Egyptian Expedition of 1798. Kléber was wounded at the taking of Alexandria, but subsequently led his division on the march into Syria and at the siege of Acre. He defeated the Turks in several actions, including the battle of Mount Tabor, where he was opposed by a much stronger force than his own.

After the secret departure of Napoleon for France in 1799, Kléber found to his rage that he had been left in command of the depleted (and unpaid) French Army. Indeed his treasury was in deficit to the sum of twelve million francs, disease and death had reduced the army to half its original strength and a newly landed Turkish Army was about to attack. It was an indication that Napoleon's famed luck was still with him that, by the time Kléber's indignant despatches reached Paris, the Directory had been overthrown and Napoleon himself installed as First Consul. In circumstances which might have disheartened the most optimistic of men, Kléber contrived to continue the fight to control Cairo and retain some ascendancy over Egypt. The Convention which General Kléber agreed with the Turks and the English under the command of Sir Sidney Smith did not find favour in London, and Kléber was compelled to continue his struggle against the Turks, gaining a notable victory at Heliopolis. It was a near-fatal

blow to the French Army, which was under attack from the native population as well from the Turks and the British expeditionary force, when he
was stabbed to death by an Arab fanatic on 14th June 1800.

He was a general who was very much respected by the troops under his
command as a man of unquestioned bravery and coolness; when at the
beginning of July 1801 the French troops under General Bélliard capitulated to the British and marched out of Cairo, they brought with them the
black draped coffin of General Kléber. His humanity and integrity have
never been doubted, although Napoleon, busily rewriting history at St
Helena, was reported to have told Gourgaud that the French Army's defeat
in Egypt was the fault of General Kléber who, he said 'was German, not
French, and unlike me did not love the Revolution'. History has been
kinder to this courageous officer. Louis XVIII on his restoration to the
throne caused Kléber's body to be re-interred in 1818 at Strasbourg, his
birthplace, with full military honours in recognition of his services to
France.

Jean Lannes, Duke of Montebello (1769–1809)

Born in the same year as Napoleon himself, Lannes enjoyed both the
friendship and respect of the Emperor. He was a soldier of enormous
courage, as his numerous wounds attested. His military service began in
1792, and he was active first in the Pyrenées, where he received a wound in
the arm, then with the Army of Italy, under Napoleon, receiving three
wounds in three days at the battle at Arcola in 1796. He was confirmed as a
General of Brigade after the capture of Mantua.

In the course of the campaign in Egypt he helped to repress the first
revolt in Cairo and accompanied Napoleon on the incursion into Syria. He
was wounded again during the assault on Acre and was shot in the leg at the
battle of Aboukir, after the return of the army to Egypt. In August 1799 he
was selected as one of the very few senior officers to return to France with
Napoleon, where he supported him as the Directory was overthrown and
Napoleon's power increased. Lannes was rewarded for his loyalty by being
appointed Inspector General of the Consular Guard and confirmed in his
rank of General of Division.

In the early days of Napoleon's consulate, Lannes enjoyed the euphoria of
the new order, attending the many receptions and parties given by Josephine
at her new home, Malmaison. But France was still at war and on 9th June
1800, Lannes, at the head of the advance guard of the Army of the Reserve,
was the victor of the battle of Montebello. Five days later at Marengo he
faced the Austrians, who outnumbered him, and resisted them so effectively
that Desaix was able to arrive with his division and save the day.

Throughout the Napoleonic era, until his death, Lannes took a prominent part in the battles of each campaign, giving repeated evidence of his skills as a field commander. His bravery and brilliance were rewarded lavishly: he was made a Marshal of France in 1804 and created Duke of Montebello in 1808. He accumulated pensions and became a rich man.

During the Spanish campaign, when he commanded a corps, he succeeded in bringing about the surrender of Saragossa in February 1809, which had resisted all attack since the previous June. Shortly afterwards he was recalled to the German theatre of war in command of the 2nd Corps of the Army of Germany. It was at the battle of Aspern-Essling, where the French suffered twenty-one thousand casualties, that Lannes sustained grave injuries towards the end of the first day from a cannonball which smashed both of his legs. The right leg was amputated, but nine days later he died. He was the first of the marshals to die in action and his loss was felt severely both by the Army, which admired him, and by Napoleon, whose friend he had been.

Like many of the soldiers born of the Revolution, Lannes had not had the support of wealth or high birth in his early days, but had benefited from the fact that many of those who had enjoyed such advantages had been eliminated by emigration or the Terror. He had chosen the military life voluntarily and had seized the opportunities it presented with determination and bravery. He was not a 'political' soldier, and was thus an ideal subordinate for Napoleon, who appreciated his reliability and battlefield courage.

The Mameluks

Although Egypt was a province of the Ottoman Empire at the time of Napoleon's Egyptian Expedition, it was in effect ruled by the Mameluk Beys, who extracted heavy tributes from the native population. The taxes they raised from the twenty-four provinces were supposed to be paid to the Sultan, but in practice all but a very small amount remained in the hands of the Beys, who had become powerful rulers of their separate kingdoms. They had dominated Egypt for over five hundred years.

Most of them were of Circassian, Georgian and Armenian ancestry, and they usually married women from those countries. As they were relatively few in number it was necessary for them to recruit their soldiers from elsewhere; this they achieved by purchasing hundreds of young boys as slaves from the Caucasus. These boys were brought up as warriors and could, if successful, gain their freedom. As soldiers the Mameluks were brave and ferocious, but as they owed no allegiance to any one leader they were undisciplined, and even their magnificent horsemanship could not

178

prevail against the steadiness of the seasoned French troops. In spite of their determined opposition to him, Napoleon admired their qualities as soldiers, even taking one of their number, a slave named Roustam, for his personal servant. In 1801 a squadron of Mameluks, in splendid oriental dress, was formed in France under French officers, remaining as part of the Imperial Guard until it was disbanded in 1814.

General Jacques François de Boussay, Baron de Menou (1750–1810)

Menou entered the French Army in 1766, was commissioned two years later, and held the rank of Colonel at the start of the Revolution. He was Deputy for the Nobility in the States-General, being an enthusiastic partisan of revolutionary ideals, and after service in the Army of the Rhine he was promoted to a General of Division. He retired from the Army in 1793, following a severe wound incurred at the taking of Samur, but was recalled in 1795 to command the Army of the Interior. In this capacity he confronted Royalist insurgents in Paris on 4th October, ordering them to disperse, which they refused to do. Menou then withdrew and was later arrested, his command being given to Barras.[105] Acquitted at his subsequent trial by a military court, he was found to be a hard worker and good administrator by Napoleon, who included him as a General in command of the 4th Division on his Egyptian expedition. Soon after landing in Egypt Menou was again wounded at the taking of Alexandria and was replaced as divisional commander by General Vial.

It was during the French occupation of Egypt that Menou converted to Islam and married an Egyptian, said to be the daughter of a bath-attendant, neither rich nor beautiful. Their son, Said Soliman Mourad Jacques Menou, was the first citizen recorded by the French in the census of Cairo. It was as a result of this apparent commitment to Egypt and the Islamic faith that, when Menou became Commander-in-Chief of the Army of Egypt following Napoleon's departure for France and the assassination of his successor General Kléber, by virtue of seniority, the Army suspected him of favouring the establishment of a French colony in Egypt, rather than negotiating their return to France.

General Menou was much blamed for the defeat of the French at Canope by a British force under General Abercromby. Prior to his surrender to the British in August 1801 there had been a considerable amount of dissension between Menou and his subordinate generals. This had approached so nearly to disobedience that the Commander-in-Chief had two of them, Generals Reynier and Damas, arrested and returned to France together

---

[105] Paul François Jean Nicolas Barras (1755–1820).

with some other less senior officers. Menou had always been a great admirer of Napoleon and had previously criticised the actions of General Kléber, claiming that they would not have been sanctioned by the first Commander-in-Chief.

Following the French surrender there were discussions regarding the ownership of the papers and artefacts which had been collected by the Commission of Science and the Arts that had accompanied the French Army. The scientists and artists were reluctant to hand over their hard-won treasures. Eventually it was decided that the learned men should keep their written work, but should hand over the artefacts, among them the Rosetta Stone. Menou, however, refused at first to surrender the Stone, claiming it to be his private property. At last, he was compelled to write to the British commander. 'You want it, Monsieur le Général? You can have it, since you are the stronger of us two . . . You may pick it up whenever you please.' A Colonel Turner came to claim the Stone, which had been stored in a warehouse in Alexandria beside Menou's personal baggage. The Rosetta Stone was shipped to England on HMS *l'Egyptienne*, a forty-four-gun vessel captured from the French.

Together with the remains of the army, General Menou was returned to France under the agreement finally signed with the British, thereafter occupying administrative posts; he was made a Count of the Empire by Napoleon in 1808.

Although apparently not deficient in physical courage, Menou's indecisiveness as a Commanding Officer could hardly have been more unfortunate in the situation in which he found himself in Egypt. His abilities as an administrator were considerable and it was greatly to his credit that during his period as Commander-in-Chief in Egypt he continued the work begun by Kléber to ensure that the troops were paid regularly and that profiteering at the Army's expense was minimised.

Gaspard Monge, Count of Pélouse (1746–1818)

This French mathematician and natural philosopher was born at Beaune in 1746. He taught mathematics and physics at the military school of Mezières and became a member of the Academy of Sciences in 1780. In 1792 he was made Minister of the Marine and was one of the founders of the *Ecole Polytechnique*. At the period when the Revolution was mobilising to meet the allied threat to its frontiers, Monge invented a new method of extracting saltpetre from the soil in order to supply the mounting requirement for gunpowder.

It was in 1796 that he was instructed to go to Italy to collect the artistic and scientific treasures from the countries conquered during Napoleon's

Italian Campaign. Among the valuables he seized for France were more than eight hundred great paintings, including the *Mona Lisa*.

When it was proposed that a Scientific Commission should accompany Bonaparte's expedition to Egypt, Monge was one of the two eminent men – Berthollet was the other – entrusted with the enrolment of the artists, technicians and scientists who would later be the members of the Institute of Egypt, of which Monge himself was to be President. When Napoleon became Emperor of the French, Monge became a senator, was created Count of Pélouse and granted an estate in Westphalia together with a the gift of two-hundred thousand francs.

An American inventor, Robert Fulton, appealed to Monge for his help in interesting the French Government in his proposal to build 'a submarine bomb or torpedo' to place under a ship, which he claimed would be so new and secret that the morale of the Royal Navy would be completely destroyed. Napoleon was influenced by Monge and a prototype, the *Nautilus*, was in fact built. She was not an unqualified success at her trials and eventually the French lost interest and Robert Fulton transferred himself and his inventions to London.

On the restoration of the monarchy, Monge was deprived of all his offices: he died in 1818. His principal written works are 'Descriptive Geometry', 'The Application of Analysis to the Geometry of Surfaces' and 'Treatise on Statistics.'

Murad Bey (1750–1801)

At the time of Napoleon's incursion into Egypt in 1798, Murad was one of the two beys, or princes, who held most of the power in that country. The other, Ibrahim, wielded influence from Cairo, while Murad governed from Ginza. Brave, cruel and greedy, these beys had for years struggled against their Turkish overlords and fought for power amongst themselves. They united, however, against the French invasion. It was Napoleon's proclaimed purpose to 'liberate' the Egyptians from the oppression of the Mameluks; at first he announced that he was the ally of the Sultan.

In spite of their courage and the splendour of their equipment, Murad and Ibrahim were routed by the superior discipline of the French at the Battle of the Pyramids, and Murad fled south into the desert. Thereafter, pursued by General Desaix, he was frequently worsted and caused to flee in battle, but he was never caught and managed to keep an army of about five thousand mounted warriors together.

He refused to cooperate with his Turkish overlords when they at last entered the battle against the French, and his loyalties became questionable. At one time the French actually appointed Murad as Governor of Upper

Egypt, but he then entered into negotiations with Sir Sidney Smith, who was seeking to land a British expeditionary force on the Red Sea coast.

When Murad died of plague in 1801 it was not clear whether he and his army were on the way to join General Belliard in Cairo or the British forces under General Hutchinson.

Colonel Louis Edmond Le Picard de Phélippeaux (1768-1799)

Phélippeaux was a fellow pupil and rival of his exact contemporary, Napoleon Bonaparte, both becoming artillery officers on leaving the *Ecole Militaire*. Phélippeaux was promoted to Captain in 1789, but as he was of aristocratic birth he was forced to emigrate in 1791, after which he served on the staff of the Prince de Condé. He campaigned with a corps of Royalists in the Vendée, where he was captured but rescued on the eve of his execution.

In 1795 he re-entered France to organise a Royalist insurrection in the central provinces. He took Sancerre, and maintained his position in Berry for some time. Afterwards he went to Paris, where he effected the liberation of Sir Sidney Smith from the Temple prison where he had been incarcerated and was in danger of execution.

Phélippeaux accompanied Sir Sidney to London, and was granted a commission in the British Army. When Sir Sidney was appointed to command the *Tigre* in 1798 and ordered to proceed with his brother as joint plenipotentiary to the Levant, he asked five Royalist officers, among them Phélippeaux, to go with him.

In Constantinople, plans were made to harass the French in Egypt, in preparation for which Phélippeaux took a commission as Colonel in the Turkish Army. In 1799 the *Tigre* arrived at Acre, which was then threatened with attack from the French, who had already laid waste El Arich, Gaza and Jaffa. It was due in great part to the skill and energy of Colonel Phélippeaux that the decayed fortifications of the strategically vital town were able to resist assault after assault by the French. The stubborn resistance of the defenders of the city outlasted Bonaparte's patience, and gave time for the losses to the French Army from death, wounds and disease to have their fatal effect. After two months Napoleon retreated, but the French Royalist colonel had, as Sir Sidney Smith wrote, 'fallen a sacrifice to his zeal for this service; want of rest and exposure to the sun having given him a fever of which he died.' It might have been this French soldier's epitaph.

Jean Louis Ebenezer Reynier (1771–1814)

Reynier was born on 14th January 1771 in Lausanne. He trained as an engineer, but joined the French Army as a gunner in 1792. In the days of the Revolutionary wars promotion was rapid and, after active service under General Charles François Dumouriez, he achieved the rank of General of Brigade. In this rank he saw service under Moreau in the Army of the Rhine, and it was as a general commanding the 2nd Division that he accompanied Bonaparte on the Egyptian expedition in 1798.

When the expedition disembarked on arrival near Alexandria, General Reynier, together with General Desaix, led the appalling march towards Cairo through the desert without water and under a burning sun. His division took part in the Battle of the Pyramids, and also in the invasion of Syria. On his return in November 1799 his name was included among the members of the Commission of Science and the Arts.

He took a prominent part in the battle at Heliopolis which provided General Kléber with a brilliant victory over the Turkish forces. Less than three months later Kléber was assassinated and General Menou became Commander-in-Chief of the remains of the French Army of Egypt. Following defeat at Canope, the new Commanding General attempted to lay the blame for the failure upon Reynier and General Damas, both of whom had been open in their criticism of him. Reynier and Damas were returned to France together with two other senior officers. Furious at the doubts which had been cast upon his honour and competence as a soldier, on his arrival back in France Reynier published a violent attack upon General Menou, which was, however, suppressed by Napoleon. This did not prevent Reynier from challenging General Destaing, who had arrested him in Egypt, to a duel and killing him.

His career was not ended by these events and in 1808 he was Minister of War in the Kingdom of Naples; thereafter he served in the Peninsula and in 1811 he was rewarded by being made a Count of the Empire. He also took part in the Russian campaign of 1812 and was present at the Battle of the Nations at Leipzig in October 1813, which effectively cost Napoleon control of Germany. Reynier was taken prisoner at this battle, where his Saxon troops defected to the allied armies. Reynier was returned to France in a prisoner exchange in 1814, where he died two weeks later.

Admiral Sir William Sidney Smith GCB (1764–1840)

The son of a disreputable army officer, John Spencer Smith was born in London in 1764. He was educated at Tonbridge School, but at the age of twelve left to join *HMS Tortoise*, first as a captain's servant, then as midshipman. After experiencing serious action on the brig *Unicorn*, he joined *Sandwich*, flagship of the Channel Fleet under Admiral Rodney.

When only nineteen, in 1783, he commanded the thirty-two-gun frigate *Alcmene* until the ship was paid off at the end of the American War of

Independence. On half-pay, Smith spent time in France, perfecting his knowledge of the language, afterwards journeying through Southern Europe and the Middle East as far as Morocco. During these travels he displayed a talent for intelligence gathering, and his reports on foreign naval installations and forces were well received by the Secretary to the Admiralty.

His potential usefulness gained him permission to visit Sweden, then at war with Russia. King Gustavus III recognised his ability and gave him command of a coastal force of four thousand marines sailing in vessels ranging from frigates to oared in-shore gunboats. Smith's success against Russian flotillas earned him a Swedish knighthood in 1790.

In 1792 he was in Constantinople serving as a volunteer officer in the Turkish Navy, and again indulging his aptitude for espionage. The outbreak of hostilities between France and England in 1793 took him to Toulon, where Admiral Hood was assisting French Royalists to defend the area against advancing Republican armies. When continued resistance became impossible Hood placed Smith in command of an operation to burn the French warships anchored in the harbour and destroy the shore installations. His success was rewarded by an appointment to command the thirty-eight-gun frigate *Diamond,* in which he carried out attacks on French coastal shipping. In April 1796 an unsuccessful attack on a French privateer resulted in Smith becoming a prisoner-of-war.

He spent the next two years in prison in Paris, accused of spying and at risk of execution. Smith owed his dramatic escape from the Temple prison to dedicated French Royalists who endangered their own lives to assist him.

Napoleon's Egyptian expedition of 1798 threatened the Ottoman empire and Smith, already familiar with the region, was ordered to the Levant to encourage the Sultan's opposition to France. He was given the command of the *Tigre,* an eighty-gun ship of the line with a hand-picked crew of six-hundred and forty men. This involved command over the whole English naval force in the Eastern Mediterranean and, after negotiations with the Sultan, command also of all Turkish naval and military forces in the area.

He made ingenious and bold use of the force he commanded. Against all probability Smith rallied the Turkish defenders to resist repeated attacks on the key fortress of Acre, compelling the French to withdraw their army, which was much reduced by disease and death. It was a crucial victory. Napoleon was denied his dreams of Eastern conquest, and the French Army of Egypt was rendered impotent. Sir Sidney Smith was the 'Hero of Acre'. He remained actively engaged in the last stages of the war in Egypt and in the protracted and confused negotiations for the final French surrender and evacuation.

The success at Acre brought him great popularity at home, a generous pension and the offer of a parliamentary seat in Rochester when he returned to London in 1801. He enjoyed a busy social life and was for a time the lover of the estranged Princess of Wales, Caroline of Brunswick.

From the renewal of war with France in May 1803 until 1814, Sir Sidney's commands were mainly in the Mediterranean. With the exception of the capture of Capri in 1806, he failed to match the spectacular successes of his early years. In 1810 he became a vice-admiral and in the same year married Caroline Rumbold, the widow of an English diplomat.

After 1814 he was never offered another command. The charming and flamboyant personality which delighted the public aroused the distrust, dislike and jealousy of his more sober naval contemporaries. Even his promotion to full admiral rank was withheld until 1821. In retirement he campaigned vigorously for the abolition of slavery worldwide, but after the death of his wife in 1826 he led a sometimes eccentric and often impecunious life in his beloved Paris until his death in May 1840.

Despite his obvious contributions to the final British victory over the French, Sidney Smith is little remembered today as one of the heroes of the Napoleonic era. Paradoxically, Nelson admired Smith as a fighting sailor, but Wellington had no time for him and is quoted as saying 'I cannot believe that a man so silly in other affairs can be a good naval officer.' In exile, however, Napoleon stated 'Sidney Smith is a brave officer ... He is active, intelligent, intriguing and indefatigable; but I believe he is half mad.'

APPENDICES

APPENDIX 1

Ships of the Expeditionary Force which left Toulon on the 29th and 30th
Floréal, Year VI [18th and 19th May, 1798], not including dispatch boats,
privateers etc.

Ships of the line
Le Mercure, 74 guns; *Le Timoléon*, 74 guns; *Le Guillaume Tell*, 80 guns; *Le
Généreux*, 74 guns; *Le Peuple Gouvernant*, 74 guns; *Le Tonnant*, 80 guns;
L'Orient, 130 guns; *L'Heureux*, 74 guns; *Le Conquérant*, 74 guns; *Le
Spartiate*, 74 guns; *Le Franklin*, 80 guns; *Le Guerrier*, 74 guns.

Frigates
La Diane, 50 guns; *L'Alceste*, 60 guns; *Le Corcyre*, 16 guns; *L'Artémise*, 40
guns; *LaFortune*, 40 guns; *La Lordi*, 40 guns; *La Sérieuse*, 40 guns; *La
Junon*, 40 guns.

Ships with light armaments
Warships: *Le Dubois, l'Alceste*.
Frigates or Brigs: *La Sensible, La Courageuse, La Mantoue, La Carrére, La
Muiron*.
La Badine: a corvette of 48 guns.

APPENDIX 2

**Members of the Egyptian Institute, established by a decree of
Bonaparte on 5th Fructidor, Year VI [22nd August, 1798]**

Mathematicians

Antoine François Andréossy (1761–1828)
Artillery general who in July 1798 commanded the French flotilla on the
Nile.

Napoleon Bonaparte (1769–1821)
Commander-in-Chief of the French Army of the Orient; first Vice-President of the Egyptian Institute.

Louis Costaz (1767–1842)

Jean Baptiste Joseph Fourier (1768–1830)
Became Permanent Secretary of the Egyptian Institute.

Pierre Simon Girard (1765–1836)

Jacques Marie Lepére (1763–1841)

Etienne Louis Malus de Mitry (1775–1812)
Distinguished engineer officer who served under Caffarelli. He became ill

of the plague while serving with Kléber during the Syrian campaign, from which he eventually recovered.

Gaspard Monge (1746–1818)
Celebrated scholar who became the first President of the Egyptian Institute and was a personal friend of Bonaparte.

Nicholas Auguste Nouët (1740–1811)

François Marie Quesnot (1761–??)

Horace Say (1771–1799)
Chief Staff Officer of the Engineers. He was wounded at Acre, his arm was amputated and he died either as a result of the amputation or of plague, which was then raging at Jaffa where he had been taken.

Jean Jacques Sebastien Leroy (1747–1825)

Physicists

Claude Louis Berthollet (1748–1822)
Accompanied Bonaparte to Egypt with a view to creating the Egyptian Institute.

Jacques Pierre Champy de Boisserand (1744–1816)

Nicolas Jacques Conté (1755–1805)
An inventor, much admired by Bonaparte. He played an important part in overseeing the production of the engravings used in the monumental 'Description of the Egyptian Expedition'.

Delisle
An alternative spelling of his name, 'Delille', appears in some sources.

Hippolyte Victor Collet des Descotils (1773–1815)

Nicolas René Dufriche Desgenettes (1762–1837)
Physician-in-Chief to the Expedition. His knowledge of military hygiene and medicine enabled him to confront the outbreak of plague at Jaffa, against which he experimentally inoculated himself and survived.

Dieudonné Guy Tancrède Dolomieu (1750–1801)
Geologist and member of the Scientific Commission.

Jean Marie Joseph Aymé Dubois (1779–1846)

Etienne Geoffroy Saint-Hilaire (1772–1844)
A celebrated zoologist.

Marie Jules César le Lorgne Savigny (1777–1851)
Zoologist who edited most of the work relating to the natural history of invertebrates in the 'Description of Egypt'.

Political Economists

Louis Marie Joseph Maximilien Caffarelli du Falga (1756–1799)
Commander of the Engineers in the Army of the Orient, appointed as a member of the Egyptian Institute in August 1798. A particular friend of Napoleon, he died following injury at the siege of Acre.

Alexis Gloutier (1758–1800)

Jean-Baptiste Poussielgue (1764–1845)

Administrator of finance in Egypt. He was active in the negotiations leading up to the Treaty of El Arich.

Jozef Sulima Sulkowski (1770[?]–1798)

One of Bonaparte's aides-de-camp in Egypt and appointed to the Egyptian Institute in August 1798. He was assassinated during the first uprising in Cairo.

Simon Antoine François Marie de Sucy (1764–1799)

Member of the Egyptian Institute from August 1798. He was wounded at the Battle of the Pyramids and was attacked and murdered when he disembarked at Sicily on the return journey to France.

Jean-Lambert Tallien (1767–1820)

Previously a member of the Committee of Public Safety and the Council of Five Hundred. He was appointed to the Egyptian Institute in August 1798 and edited the *Egyptian Decade* at Cairo. Returning to France in October 1800 he was captured by the English but soon set at liberty.

Literature and the Arts

Dominique Vivant Denon (1747–1825)

His drawings and descriptions of Egyptian antiquities provided some of the most remarkable material in the 'Description of Egypt', published between 1809 and 1822.

Andre Dutertre (1753–1842)

The Expedition's leading artist. He provided portraits of the members of the Institute and of many of the officers of the Expedition.

Charles Norry (1756–1832)

Françoise Auguste Parseval-Grandmaison (1759–1834)
Poet.

Henri Joseph Redouté (1766–1852)

Don Raphaël
A Greek priest.

Henri Jean Rigel (1772–1852)

Jean-Michel Venture de Paradis (1739–1799)
Distinguished orientalist who became the chief interpreter for the Expedition. He succumbed to illness in May 1799.

The first meeting of this Institute took place on 6th Fructidor, Year VI [23rd August 1798]. Monge was chosen as President and Bonaparte as Vice-President. The Institute rendered great service to the Army, providing the techniques by which bread was baked, beer brewed and Nile water purified, as well as the means to manufacture gunpowder.

APPENDIX 3

Notes taken from a private letter concerning the generals on the Expedition, dated 23rd May 1800.

General Caffarelli, who was killed at the siege of St Jean-d'Acre, was one of the most meritorious and scholarly of men. His knowledge of engineering had made him extremely valuable to the Army, but as he was supposed (wrongly) to have advocated the Egyptian expedition the soldiers seem to have disliked him. The General was lame – he had a wooden leg. The gibe, 'It's all right for him to go to Egypt – he'll always have one leg in France', was often repeated. Caffarelli had such control of the men he commanded at St Jean-d'Acre that he led them fourteen times to the attack, a circumstance unprecedented in the accounts of sieges. He died courageously at last.

Among the total of human follies must be counted the marriage of Monsieur, the Baron de Menou, who married the daughter of a bath attendant. It was not wealth, nor beauty, nor love which led to this idiocy. His wife – so the letter states – was nineteen years old and very ugly with a square, flat figure, her skin dark, and she had an empty mind; nevertheless, for the sake of some six hundred thousand francs which she possessed he forgot everything which might have restrained him, became a Turk, even to the point of being circumcised, and turned Mohammedan.

Among the manifestations of savage courage must be numbered the exploits of the famous Greek, Barthelémy who, alone, attacked and overcame seven Bedouins, cutting off their heads and tying them around his horse. It is difficult to imagine a man who could swim two hundred yards against a current which threatened to engulf him, seize an Arab *chebec*[106] carrying sixteen men and drag it to the bank despite all opposition. These are only samples of a thousand other exploits.

A French officer was taken prisoner by the Bedouins, who subjected him to the cruellest of all shames for a man before having him led away. His wife was present. The tears and cries of this miserable woman did nothing to halt the lechery of these wretches. The French recaptured this officer. His

---

[106] A narrow, three-sailed boat.

197

wife was in despair; she recounted her experience, or rather that of her husband, in these strange words 'These monsters, not content with all their other stupidities, had to take my unhappy husband ... the devils, the villains. I offered myself to them, but they preferred their beastliness and took a poor man of fifty years old.' That is an example of the ways of the desert barbarians.

INDEX

Names in the text